"PAUL HOOD'S BOOK
IS A MUST READ."

- JIM STOVALL
(New York Times Best-Selling Author and
Emmy Award-Winning Entrepreneur)

ROADKILL TASTES LIKE CHICKEN

PAUL HOOD

FOREWORD
FOREWORD BY JIM STOVALL:

I first met Paul Hood when his accounting firm purchased the CPA firm I had been dealing with for many years. Paul is an accountant, but much more, he is an entrepreneur. I have spoken for his firm, and he and I began meeting regularly as he pursued a multi-state, multi-firm expansion of his business. Paul Hood performs like an accountant but thinks like an entrepreneur. When my wife and I funded the Stovall Center for Entrepreneurship at Oral Roberts University here in our hometown of Tulsa, Oklahoma, I took it upon myself to see that our students from around the world were exposed to great entrepreneurs. Steve Forbes did a video presentation for the ribbon-cutting, and we have had a succession of world-class entrepreneurs come through the Stovall Center. No one has been more giving of their time, experience, and expertise than Paul Hood. He can speak to college students aspiring to be business owners about both accounting principles and the art of entrepreneurship.

I have written over 50 books, and 8 of them have been turned into movies. One of my late, great business partners was fond of saying, "If you can tell a great story, you earn the right to share your message." Within these pages, Paul Hood will definitely earn the right to share his powerful success messages with you. If I had written his story as one of my novels or as a script for one of our movies, it would have been instantly rejected as unbelievable. You may have heard it said that we all start at ground zero. This may be true, but a lot of people like Paul Hood, had to struggle and do a lot of intense work just to elevate themselves to ground zero. One of my favorite authors, Louis L'Amour once said, "No one can be judged except against the backdrop of the time and place in which they lived. "

As you read and re-live Paul's story, you will have access to his perspective. He made sacrifices to learn some extremely valuable principles and fought hard to implement them in his life. Opportunities come disguised as problems. We learn from adversity—either our own or the experience that others share with us.

Paul, through this book, gives you and I the opportunity to learn, grow, and benefit from his experiences without going through the pain and anguish he experienced. I believe that when you turn the last page, you will have a new perspective and a new vision for the possibilities within your own life. You will have a heightened sense of gratitude for the opportunities you've been given, and you will be forever changed for the better. Read, learn, and succeed. – Jim Stovall, 2022

TESTIMONIALS

"Paul Hood is proof that the American Dream is still alive and available for those that are willing to be diligent and have a never give up attitude. In a day where it is not only easy but accepted to have a victim mentality, Paul details in his book the things he learned on his path from poverty to ultra-success in an effort to take away excuses and light the path for others to follow. If you want more out of life, grab his book, Road Kill Tastes Like Chicken."

MARKWAYNE MULLIN

Serial Entrepreneur and current United States Senator representing the State of Oklahoma

"I met Paul through a mutual friend that suggested I have him on my show to give his testimony. His story of poverty to success brought tears to all of our eyes. His story includes many points where the hand of God was very active and his greatest victory was submitting to God's vision for his life. This book is a must read story of triumph. Paul's testimony can be seen at https://youtu.be/k41eXD0lZko"

PASTOR DAVID SCARLETT

Founder of the worldwide ministry His Glory, https://hisglory.me/

"I have learned through struggles in my life growing up in Brooklyn that success is generally how you react to what life throws at you. My friend Paul chose to take adversity and turn it into energy to change his life. Through his book Road Kill Tastes Like Chicken, Paul is sharing how all of us can do the same."

COACH MIKE BOYNTON

Men's Head Basketball Coach at Oklahoma State University

"Paul Hood's story is proof you can gain common sense from uncommon circumstances and when you are a victim of hardship, it doesn't mean you are a victim. I've known Paul for years and he doesn't just talk about being positive or generous or seeing problems as opportunities, he lives it every day. And, he didn't wait for his life to be rosy, he adopted that mindset when he was surrounded by addiction, crime and poor choices. He chose not to be defined by his circumstances and to create his own American dream story. It's a story filled with faith, hard work, sacrifice, laughter, tears and inspiration. I know I'm a better person for knowing Paul and I believe you will be better for reading his story. You will find truth and encouragement and will be ready to write your own American dream story, complete with an ending of your choosing."

LORI FULLBRIGHT

Two-time Emmy award winner news anchor for the CBS affiliate in Tulsa OK and a honoree in the 50th Annual Oklahoma Journalism Hall of Fame

"I've known Paul Hood since little league football and I've always loved his courage and persistence to win. Paul has always been a fearless competitor despite being one of the smallest players on the team. In this book, he shows through perseverance and God's help, how he overcame life's difficulties and turned a bad situation around. "

MITCH NASH

Co-captain of the Oklahoma State Football Team, 4-year varsity letterman as running back. Retired US Army receiving the Defense Meritorious Service Medal, Meritorious Service Medal, Joint Service Commendation Medal, Army Commendation Medal, Joint Service Achievement Medal, Army Achievement Medal, Army Good Conduct Medal, National Defense Service Medal, Global War on Terrorism Service Medal, and the Korean Defense Service Medal

"From the time we met Paul we knew how driven he was to succeed. Paul never slows down, never stops, and never ceases to amaze us with the things he's able to accomplish. This book is jam packed with Paul's heart, wisdom, and encouragement! After you read Paul's story, you're going to be inspired to take your life to the next level in all areas. Paul has been our accountant, financial advisor, and friend for over 16 years. He has helped us grow from an in-home personal training studio to a multi-million-dollar chain of fitness centers in the U.S. His drive, vision, and can-do attitude has helped push us to reach new goals we set. Paul has cheered us on, challenged us to set the bar higher, and celebrated with us at the end. Over the years we've watched Paul give so much of himself to help others reach their goals as well. He spends countless hours giving away advice on the local TV news station, radio stations, hosting free financial seminars, and writing books. He sees potential in everyone. He doesn't try to over complicate things and will continue to explain a concept until you understand. Paul wants to take you to the next level of success and this book will do just that."

CHARLES & AMBER COLAW

The original owners and founders of the multi-state chain of gyms operated as Colaw Fitness. https://colawfitness.com/our-story/

"What can I say about Paul Hood? So many things have impressed me from the first time I met Paul, to our car scene activities, to our couple dinners and our talks about business. The thing that has really impressed me is his knowledge of business. I have dealt with so many accountants and CPA's over the years. They have all pretty much been the same until I met Paul. He just decided one day that he wasn't going to settle "just being" an accountant. He decided to be a businessman, build an amazing business, and create a life that will continue for generations! I was so excited about the opportunity to read Paul's book. I had already heard a lot of the stories and advice that are in this book and I can't wait until everyone gets to hear his perspective. Paul has worked hard, made sacrifices and has implemented a successful business plan to get him where he is today. In this book you will learn about the struggles, Taking action, Handling money, who to surround yourself with, giving back and family. In my opinion there is not a better person that could tell this story and anyone that reads it will be better off."

JOHN EDDIE HALL

Partner in over 20 Domino's franchise locations doing more than 30 million dollars in volume and owning more than 20 million dollars in real estate.

"I've known Paul for many years and it's been an honor having him as a mentor and friend. His contribution to my life has been enlightening and pivotal in my own personal growth. His personal life experiences, coaching, wisdom, and guidance have helped to change the lives of so many. Paul has gone from a place of poverty to a place of prosperity while maintaining character and integrity which is absolutely incredible! He is using his own personal achievement and wealth as a seed to equip, empower, and inspire others to rise above the difficulties and limitations of life and become the best version of themselves. I can see this through his countless efforts in helping those in need and financially supporting numerous charity organizations including Gibraltar Youth. Gibraltar Youth is a program that focuses on empowering young people in the lower income areas to bravely face and overcome their obstacles, and ultimately set them on a path to becoming successful adults-- thereby breaking the cycle of poverty, ignorance, and abuse that often plagues today's youth. This is what Paul's story is all about; life-changing for all who read it. One candle in the midst of a very dark room always makes a difference, because hope is what we need-- this is the impact Paul's book will have. Through this book, he is inspiring the young and old to develop purpose, perspective, and ultimately the ability to arrive at a better tomorrow."

EKE ENIS

Founder and Director of Gibraltar Youth, mentoring, inspiring young minds, preaching the gospel with a passion for inspiring the youth of North Tulsa. Co-Pastor of the Ministry of Reconciliation Church and co-owner of ECS Electric.

"Paul has been a fighter all of his life. This book is another example of where he demands us to lean in on our challenges and to take ownership and accountability for them. A must read for those wanting a change in their personal path in life."

MARTY SCHOENTHALER

Experienced top executive roles at some of the largest companies in the US including CEO of Tate Boys Tires, VP and CIO of Archer Daniels Midland and GM of Corporate Information Technology at ConcoPhillips Corporation

"When I think of Paul Hood a couple things stand out to me. First, he has created something from nothing. He did not inherit money or a business, but instead created first generation wealth which is very inspiring. Second, he has mental and physical self-control. Paul did a Physique Body Building show at the age of 50 with his son. The ability to execute, be consistent and intentional is a skill that few people possess."

DR ROBERT ZOELLNER

Optometrist and entrepreneur growing more than a dozen startups to multi-million dollar business's.

"My husband and I are both CPA'S in Tulsa, OK. We had the opportunity to meet Paul Hood professionally several years ago. Since then, we have known him as a business colleague and have done successful business collaborations, and transactions with him, always finding him to be a pleasure to work with, professional and trustworthy. But a family tragedy that we experienced several months ago took our professional relationship to another level. Paul's outreach to our family and the level of kindness and compassion that he shared with us was amazing. His faith and generosity to others is an example of the depth of his character and the way he lives his life. I hope his book can serve as a source of inspiration to others, since we were the beneficiaries of his kindness and compassion at the most difficult time in our lives, he certainly was an inspiration to us."

ANN FIELDS, CPA

CPA and Ann Fields, CPA

ISBN 979-8-9864278-6-7
Roadkill Tastes Like Chicken

©Copyright 2023

Published by Thrive Publishing
3920 W 91st Street South
Tulsa, OK 74132

All rights reserved. No part of this publication may be reproduced, distributed, or transmitted in any form or by any means, including photocopying, recording or other electronic or mechanical methods, without the prior written permission of the publisher, except in the case of brief quotations embodied in the critical reviews and certain other noncommercial used permitted by copyright law. For permission requests, write the publisher at the address below.

Unless otherwise noted, all scripture quotations are taken from the Living Bible (TLB) copyright 1971 by Tyndale House Foundation. Used by permission of Tyndale House Publishers, Inc., Carol Stream, Illinois 60188. All rights reserved. The Living Bible, TLB and the The Living Bible logo are registerd trademarks of Tyndale House Publishers.

Printed in the United States of America.

ROADKILL TASTES LIKE CHICKEN

Stop Making Excuses and Start Making Choices

TABLE OF CONTENTS

INTRODUCTION

INTRODUCTION

"We all won the ovarian lottery just
being born in this country"
-Warren Buffet

Hello my new friends. My name is Paul Hood, and I am a Certified Public Accountant that has created wealth and am living the "American Dream." I am also the only person in my family who hasn't spent time in jail. My dad was incarcerated multiple times, and my mom even spent almost 2 years in federal prison. You know you're a bad ass when your mom spent time in jail.

We were so poor that it was not uncommon for us to eat roadkill. I was born with a hole in my heart. I almost died from spinal meningitis when socialized medicine sent me home with a diagnosis of "tired from swimming". My Native American father died at 53 from complications of alcoholism. Pretty much every person on both sides of my family were either being abused or being abusive. Virtually none of my family (aunts, uncles, cousins, grandparents) graduated high school. Most of my family worked harder at staying on welfare than they did at being successful (It is amazing how many "disabled" people on Social Security that are in my family... haha what are the odds?).

I grew up in my early years fighting, stealing, drinking, and smoking pot. I have a scar between my eyes from an aluminum baseball bat and a scar on my forehead from a lead pipe. I have never gone to the same school in my entire life for more than two years. I am a product of alcoholism, abuse, slothfulness, and a welfare mindset.

But, this is America and we all grew up hearing or reading about how people struck it rich, dreaming and wishing that story could be ours. Is this rags-to-riches opportunity still available in America? Is there some pattern to success to help facilitate such a story? Where can a person learn this pattern if it exists? Do I have to be super lucky or be born with some massive God given talent? Does it take some special ability to achieve ultra-success? Does my family history, my heritage, my education level, the color of my skin, etc. have anything to do with my chances for success?

The journey we are about to go on together will answer these questions and more. Prepare yourself though, because you will quickly realize there is no magic to success in this story, you will read of my personal journey from poverty in Northeastern Oklahoma to a millionaire who created sustained wealth many times over. The simplicity of my path may even be such that you struggle to believe it. This is not a get rich quick book, but a get rich simple book. I'm asking you to try and erase all your preconceived thoughts about how people become successful in life. We tend to see success as a destination. When we see or meet people that are successful, we naturally think they were lucky to somehow accomplish something that we can't, or were given a "leg up" that isn't available to the rest of us. I hope by telling you my story and giving you some specific things to do, you will be encouraged and gain excitement to start your personal journey to success. As Warren Buffet says, "we all won the ovarian lottery being born in this country." To cash in the lottery winnings available to us all often requires a person to rethink how they see themselves, have intense perseverance, and an intentional plan.

There is, however, a secret to success. I often wondered as my journey progressed why I wasn't taught the basic principles of success in high school or in college or at the multi-national CPA firm I worked for. What I discovered is often times the highest educated people are the least successful. I do not know if they complicate things so much they cannot see the proverbial forest for the trees or if they pursue knowledge to a point that such pursuit becomes more important than application of what they have learned. Regardless, after you read this book, like it or not, your success or lack thereof will be totally up to you. No more excuses, no more pity parties, no more blaming others, and no more victim mentality. If you are willing to work hard, be focused and intentional, take ownership of your weaknesses and not let anything or anyone pull you down, YOU WILL ACHIEVE YOUR DREAMS.

Know this, I am not a professional writer, and this is not a book of theory. This is a synopsis of my life journey to date and the twelve things that I believe you need to know that could change your life if you CHOOSE to follow. I beg your forgiveness in advance for my writing style, for my bluntness, and if anything I say offends you.

> "I am here only to be truly helpful. I am here to represent the one who sent me. I do not have to worry about what to say or what to do because the one who sent me will direct me. I am content to be wherever, knowing the sender goes with me"
>
> **-Healer's Prayer from A Course in Miracles**

Chapter 1:

IF YOU HAD STRUGGLES GROWING UP YOU GET TO CHOOSE WHETHER THEY ARE A BLESSING OR A CURSE

"God will not make his work
made manifest by cowards"
-Ralph Waldo Emerson

I was born August 2, 1967 at the Claremore Indian Hospital in Claremore, Oklahoma. As most people know, the Cherokee people (my people) were forced to walk in horrible conditions to be relocated to Oklahoma and a large portion died on the way. The state of Oklahoma aptly named it "The Trail of Tears." The Federal government, I guess from its guilt, later established socialized medicine facilities for Native Americans. Although such facilities are significantly better today since the Tribes took over from the Bureau of Indian Affairs back in the 60's, such facilities were not remotely known for top notch medical care.

My mother was primarily Irish, but my father was one half American Indian. Back in those days, even for Oklahoma mixed raced couples were a thing to be ashamed of by some people. I will talk a lot about my parents in this book as a foundation of what I think the most important determining factors of success are and are not. My father was a very proud, loving, and affectionate man. But like a large percentage of native men, he struggled to fit into the white man's society.

My dad, like his dad, was an alcoholic. He struggled with this addiction his entire life including being completely drunk when he died in April of 1998 at the age of 53. My wife and I were in a hotel in Tennessee having just spoke at an Amway leadership conference when I received the call. He was at my grandmother's home very drunk but reading his bible when he fell over on the floor. My Grandmother and Uncle, who were both there, assumed he had just passed out like he had done so many times before, but in reality he had suffered a heart attack. My dad was very soft and sweet when sober, but was backwards and somewhat uncomfortable around people. His native reluctance to join into much of the white man's world and his alcoholism kept him from really ever having what any of us today would call a normal life. He virtually never had much of a job, he played no role in my life other than maybe seeing him a few days in the summer. He was not at my wedding, never coached or even saw me play any sports. My dad never took me or picked me up from school, was not at my high school graduation, at the birth of any of my children, or at any of my children's weddings, etc. All my father gave me is a heritage I am very proud of, a turquoise ring, and a 410 shotgun.

He did nothing to teach me how to be a man, how to defend myself, how to be a father or a husband, or how to be successful in business. My dad never played catch with me, cheered me on, celebrated any successes, or consoled me for any of the losses I suffered. I have never given my dad a "high-five," or a "chest bump". I've never ran and jumped into his arms when I needed his protection. I experience none of the normal things that a dad does with his son. As I write this, I fight tears of loss that I never heard him say he is proud of me, or job well done or dust me off and tell me to live to fight another day. I long even today for him to be proud of me and to see the man I have become. Any boy who grows up without a father in his life probably, like me, does not realize the extent of what he missed out on until he has children of his own. Being a father is about the most incredible thing any man can experience. The joy that I have experienced in doing all the things with my sons that my dad did not do with me are immeasurable. They also massively enhanced the hole that I have in my heart knowing what I missed out on. Although I wish things would have been different, I know my strength and tenacity today comes from these struggles. As Ralph Waldo Emerson stated "God will not have his work made manifest by cowards." The one thing I can say is, I have never been a coward and I have never shied away from a challenge or a fight.

My father, like his father and brother, was also physically abusive when he was drunk. He was two completely different men whether he was sober or drunk. I have seen him do things that no young boy should ever see. I saw a gentle loving tender man turn into a raging mad man. I do not know what demons he had inside him that were let out when the inhibitions were turned loose with liquor. He spent his life living on the street, in prison, living at my grandmother's house or staying with friends. I have no memory of my dad ever having a home of his own other than a trailer house on my grandmother's property long after I was grown. I greatly love my dad and understand he had massive battles to fight, but deep inside me I know he chose his life with alcohol instead of me. I do not doubt that he loved me just not enough to fight for more. I tell you all these things not to make any excuse or to taint your view of my dad but simply to give you context of where I came from.

My mother was a saint in my eyes at the time of her death in 2020 from Cancer at the age of 71, but her early years were spent as a wild young woman. She grew up with a Pentecostal preacher as a father who drank and whose discipline bordered on abuse. Her Pentecostal church believed that every time you sinned you were going to hell and had to continually earn the salvation that Jesus died for. Because you are taught that every time you even have a bad thought you are sinning, you are in a constant state of fear that your path to Heaven is contingent upon being sin free the moment you die. You literally gain and lose your salvation many times a day and just hope at the time of your death you were on the good side of being forgiven. As such, like many other preacher's kids, when my mom graduated from high school she rebelled from the church and "enjoyed" what life had to offer including marrying a dark skinned Native American man.

My mom and dad divorced when I was young, and she went on to marry 5 more times finally getting one to stick in her 40's to whom she remained married to for about 30 years until her death. Prior to her last marriage, my mom spent a ton of time working multiple jobs but also enjoying the opportunity to go out drinking frequently. As the oldest son I often would be responsible for getting my brothers up and fed and off to school or daycare. I have memories of pushing my youngest brother in a stroller to daycare then getting myself and my other brother to school. My mom would take me to "beer joints" when I was between 8 and 12 years old, I can close my eyes and smell the liquor tainted breath of older ladies getting in my face and telling me I was cute. I can still remember the cloud of cigarette smoke filled rooms, the sound of juke boxes playing music, people being loud and laughing, as well as the constant clanging of pool table balls. My mom would literally allow me to shoot shot guns at targets surrounded by drunk men and women in what was called turkey shoots at the bars. The object was to cover the target the best to win a turkey. I did win my share, but a gun and a bunch of drunks was not a great environment for any one, especially a young boy.

My mom, because of her father, was a stern disciplinarian. It was not uncommon for me to get spanked, slapped in the face, on the back, or wherever her hand landed. She seemed to hold me to a higher standard than my brothers. I was the oldest and should know better were words I heard often even at an early age. We spent a lot of time with my mom's siblings and my cousins. I hope the statute of limitations has gone up since, haha, because I learned how to smoke Marijuana holding a "joint clip" and through a "bong" at a very early age. Not having a father figure in my life, I watched and learned acceptable behavior from my older cousins. They taught me how to fight, smoke weed, shop lift, and other ways to act to take what I wanted.

The life I had with my mom forced me to grow up and act like a man much sooner that I should have. I have literally woke up to the sound of my aunt being thrown down the stairs at my house by a man that was so huge and covered with hair he looked like a grizzly bear. This same bear of a man went after my mom with a knife that same night and me as a preteen boy had to try and stop him. I remember him laughing as he threw me against the wall like a rag doll and me later crying in my room when I could let the fear out instead of having to be the man of the house and protect my mom. My youth was full of fighting and getting into trouble. I have had my head split open from a baseball bat between my eyes. I have a scar on the top of my head from a lead pipe. I have had fights with boys twice my size, fights in my front yard, fights at parks with multiple kids, fights on black top playgrounds, and shamefully even punched a girl once (she did call my mom a tomato though soooo).

Growing up being poor meant we moved around a lot. My mom would work really hard but often could not pay her rent. I have never in my life gone to the same school for more than two years. I have no place in my memory of a "home". The only consistent place that I knew would be there was my grandmother's home, (dad's mom) where we went every summer for at least two weeks.

Moving around and changing schools all the time made it hard to make friends. At one point I was the only "white" kid in my class. My wife tells stories of classmates and school teachers that she remembers. My memories center around where I got in fights, where my friends and I broke in to steal Little Debbie snack cakes (again I hope statute of limitation has gone up since), to waking up laying face up in a river stream from passing out drunk. My childhood stories mostly consisted of seeing my mom sitting on men's laps at bars, seeing my dad passed out drunk, seeing my dad smack around women and the fear in their eyes from him.

People tend to use their past as an excuse to justify their current situation or lack of success. The Bible talks about generational curses. It implies that the sins of the father are bore by his sons. I believe this means we tend to duplicate the behaviors of our parents. My dad's family has a repeated history of alcoholism and physical abuse. My mom was the only person that I know of in her family to graduate high school. Almost all of her family dropped out of high school, were abusive or were abused in their relationships, and spent more time trying to get free benefits from the government than trying to better themselves.

Mr. Michael Levine, a P.R. consultant to most of the stars in Hollywood and major political players like Obama and Bush, told me at a financial workshop I was sponsoring that "Success in life is how you play the cards you are dealt. If you are born on third base you didn't hit a triple." My mom was dealt a hand of cards that for almost everyone else in her family meant trying to "play" the system to minimize effort and maximize handouts. She is my hero because she said no to the cards she was dealt and completely changed the course of history for me and my children. She graduated high school, divorced an abusive man, raised three boys on her own, and used the social system as a hand up and not a hand out for life. She learned a trade and eventually started her own business while working a fulltime job. She literally went from food stamps to self-sustaining while raising my brothers and me.

My mother, Thomasa Carol Davenport, was the architect of my success. If she had not changed the entire path that was laid out for her by her family history and expectations, I absolutely would not be writing this book. I would have continued on like most of my family and would have spent time in prison, been an alcoholic and probably become an abusive person. Reread that because that is the focus of this entire book. You have choices regardless of your past, regardless of your economic status, and regardless of the color of your skin. Your choices have consequences that affect not only you but also potential generations to come. My mom blazed a new path for me to pick up her torch and go even further. I am the first person to graduate from college in my family and guess what...all three of my sons graduated from college. I am about the only person in my family to not have spent time in jail or in prison (including my mother) and thankfully my kids have continued this trend, haha. I grew up poor with stories of literally eating roadkill to now I live in a 25,000 sq ft home with a million dollars worth of cars in my garage. Yes I have worked hard and earned everything I have, but I also have zero doubt in my mind that had my mom not made the amazingly difficult choices and paid the price she did, I would have none of what I have or be able to give back the way I do now.

My mother literally broke the chains of poverty, alcoholism, abuse, slothfulness, and lack of education. She CHOSE to change her life and finish school. She chose not to accept being an abused wife and chose to earn what she was given. The consequences of her choices created a ripple effect that will long be felt in her lineage and my great, great, great grandkids will owe a large portion of their success to her choices.

If you have struggles in life regardless of what they are you can use them as an excuse to be unsuccessful or as energy for change. Pastor TD Jakes did a sermon about any time God gets ready to do something he starts with the power of one. "Everything starts with one. Whether it is on Nelson Mandela, one woman who refuses to give up her seat on a bus, or one person who decides we should be able to fly, or one person who invents the telephone. You have to decide if you are going to be the one or are you going to be the person who is always waiting on someone. Whenever the enemy knows that the one is coming he always sets traps to stop them from succeeding because they are the one." My courageous mom decided that she was the one!

Are you the one? The one to change your life and the lives of those you love? I believe everyone that reads this book is the one if you choose to be the one! TD Jakes also said "Strength is developed through resistance." I used to tell my sons when I coached them in football that in a dog fight one of the dogs is going to eventually roll over and pee on themselves in submission. Some people, when faced with adversity choose to get stronger and learn and some will choose to roll over and pee on themselves and play the blame game. I am nothing special but have created something special not because of my amazing talent nor from luck. I am who I am because of choices my mom made, I pay attention and have a curiosity of what made other people successful, learning from their mistakes to accelerate my success, I refuse to quit, and I work hard. Success is a learned activity requiring most of us to reshape our attitudes, pull away from our past, and learn the principles of being intentional.

SUCCESS IS A LEARNED ACTIVITY!!!

I was told a story one time that you may have heard before. Two men were walking on a beach that was covered with star fish that had washed up on the beach. There were thousands just laying on the sand dieing because they were no longer in the life-giving water. One of the men was picking them up one by one throwing them back in the ocean. His friend looked at him and asked why are you doing that? You are not going to make a difference, there are so many of them. Looking back at his friend the first man said, well I made a difference for that one. My hope and prayer for you is that you will gain the understanding and belief that YOU ARE THE ONE if you want to be, and that you have the greatness inside you to be as successful as you want to be. YOU are the only limiting factor on your path to ultra-success. I am figuratively throwing you back in the water with my success story and a pattern for a successful life for you. What you do with it is up to you. You get to choose if you are a victim of your past or was your past the resistance that strengthen you! Time to stop making excuses and start making choices. Choose to learn! Choose to work! Choose to overcome! Choose to refuse to quit! Choose to be an architect of change for your life and the lives of generations to come!

STEP #1: REALIZE YOUR PAST STRUGGLES MAKE YOU STRONG AND ARE NOT AN EXCUSE TO FAIL.

||||||||||||||||||||||||||||||||||||||||||||||||||||||||||||||||||||||

Chapter 2:

YOUR ATTITUDE IS MORE IMPORTANT THAN YOUR APTITUDE

"Knowing who you are I am
honored that you love me"
-Thomasa Davenport
(Mother of Paul Hood and
generational curse breaker)

In today's America we are infested with broke thinking as a result of victim and entitlement attitudes. If you think someone is holding you back or you are entitled to anything, you need to do some deep soul searching. You are the only person holding you back and frankly you are not entitled to anything except the opportunity to succeed. The opportunity to succeed and create unlimited income is a blessing available to you from God, simply by you being born here or living here now. No other country on the planet is truly based upon a free enterprise system. Our entire economic system is contingent on people like you taking risks for the chance at a better life. If you have a desire to succeed and are willing to work, the foundation of your success is how you see yourself and the world around you.

What do you think is the most important quality needed to be successful? It is your attitude! Napoleon Hill in his amazing bestselling book Think and Grow Rich said "Both poverty and riches are the offspring of thought". Said another way.... If you think you can, you can and if you think you can't, you can't! If I had the proverbial genie in the bottle and I had one wish to make mankind better, it would be to remove the limiting power of our brains to question our potential greatness. The way we see ourselves is primarily developed by our parents. I know, I know, most of the times when we see TV shows of people laying on a doctor's couches discussing their issues, it always starts with the parents!! In this case it is very true. The way our parents see us and the expectations they created for us is formed by how they hold us accountable and the areas in our lives that they show us affirmation. My business coach and former Entrepreneur of the year, Clay Clark, taught me "You measure what you treasure." The areas of your life where your parents or parent edified you when you succeeded and got upset with you when you underperformed, form the expectations that you place on yourself and your future.

In his amazing book The Ultimate Sales Machine, Chet Holmes says most successful people have an over doting parent. He said "if I told my mom I was going to be a bank robber, she would say baby you will be the best bank robber ever." Read that again! Chet's mom set him up to be successful in any area he chose! My mom said, "knowing who you are, I am honored that you love me"! My heart and confidence almost exploded when she said that to me. She used to also say "I wish I could buy you for what you are worth and sell you for what you think you are worth." Haha, it is her fault that statement is true. My point is you as a child are like a seedling and your parents were watering the soil. How you perceive yourself and the expectations for success are either nurtured or minimized by your parents. If you did not experience such a parent, it is not too late. The first step toward success is to change your thoughts about yourself.

Chet Holmes also mentions what he terms a reticular activating system as a filter in our brain that controls what is allowed to enter our immediate thoughts. Have you ever bought a green car and you don't remember ever seeing a green car but after you buy yours you see green cars everywhere? Or, have you ever walked outside with a group of people and one person sees a beautiful flower and another person sees a big pile of dog crap? The answer as to why both of these happen is that your brain filters out the things you teach it are not important and allows in what you trained it to focus on. You cannot lie to your subconscious. When you say something like "I am terrible at remembering names" guess what, you will be terrible at remembering names. Your self-talk is extremely important to train your reticular activating system what is true and important. I am not one of those motivational people that believe that just by speaking something it will happen but there is significant science and proof that you can change your attitude which can significantly change your future.

I have a couple questions for you to ponder. Do you think African American kids are better athletes than other races? Do you think that Asian kids are smarter than other races? Before you answer consider this. I spent many years coaching all three of my sons in football and other sports. I will admit that on the first day of practice when all my players would walk on to the field for the first time I would immediately and often subconsciously evaluate these boys. Without them even taking one snap or making a tackle, If I see three African American boys, I instantly think they are good athletes. I have a higher expectation of success for them. I spend more time on them and put them in more situations to be successful.

Wrong or right, I have for whatever reason a higher expectation for them to succeed in athletics. I edify them and jump their butts more than other players. I have seen their parents often react the same. They are celebrated when they have success, and equally as important, are chastised when they do not perform up to the expectations. Coming from the poor side of town, my experience is the expectations for success placed on them in athletics are often higher than in other areas of their lives and thus they tend to excel more in athletics. I believe the same for oriental kids. Their parents tend to place higher expectations on them in the area of academics than other areas like athletics. They are celebrated for their successes in the classroom and chastised for underperforming. Obviously, I have no formal training in this area so take all that as merely a thought exercise.

My contention is if you want kids to be successful in certain areas of life praise them for their efforts in those areas and hold them accountable when they don't work hard. You are teaching them that these areas of life are important. The opposite is also the case. The areas in their lives that you do not praise and punish them in are not important to you or to them. This is not just for kids it is for employees, friends etc. Again, WE MEASURE WHAT WE TREASURE!! So if expectations can play such a huge role in success in athletics or academics can't it be concluded that the same applies to financial success in your life? If you are blessed to have had parents or a parent that built in you the idea that you could be successful in anything you do, outstanding. If you weren't so blessed it isn't too late!!!

Francis P Martin wrote a book titled Hung by The Tongue, in which he lays out that how we think and speak literally creates success or failure. It is a biblical based book that quotes scripture detailing the power of our spoken words. Even if you are not a faith-based person the teachings in this book will change your life if you allow it. We discussed that a lot about the way we see ourselves and our future is developed by our parents or other adults in our lives. The great news is you can plant the seeds of greatness inside yourself. In his book, Martin, compares the words we say as well as the words we hear to planting crops in our minds. If you plant corn in a field, you get corn. If you want corn but you plant tomatoes no matter how much you want corn you are not getting it. You have to make a conscious CHOICE to control your thoughts and words as they relate to you and your future. Choose to fill your mind and subconscious with books, music, self-talk to intentionally change how you think. If you have negative thoughts about yourself, your potential, your future, stop and immediately ask yourself why am I putting this garbage on me. Change those thoughts to be the opposite and take intentional steps on how to improve in that area. If you have the thought "I can't remember names" come into your head, do not allow it to stay. Change the thought to "I am great at remembering names." Repeat this self-talk over and over again but also research how to better remember names, practice remembering names, read books on remembering names. Please understand I am not saying that not being able to remember names isn't real. I am saying that it is a choice to plant that seed in your mind and a choice to take deliberate steps to improve this skill. We all accept that we can get stronger through exercising our muscles. Why not accept that we can gain mental strength by exercising our minds.

Be careful here because if you are intentional about making a choice to improve, you will take away your excuse to not being successful. You will realize it is no ones fault that you aren't successful. The color of your skin or where you grew up or anything else from your past has nothing to do with your lack of success in the future. Evaluate consciously EVERY WORD AND EVERY THOUGHT. Record yourself speaking and listen to the words you say in everyday life. I know this sounds weird but how bad do you want to be successful? How bad do you want to change the path of your life and the lives of your family? You think I am kidding but I am not. If you want to lose weight eat differently and exercise. If you want to be successful and improve your attitude about yourself change the way you think and speak. Record yourself in everyday situations. Be very present in your thoughts. Change the words you speak and think and you will change your life!

What is stopping you from making drastic changes in your life? For most people it is fear and lack of faith in what can happen. I have financial workshops every other month where I bring in successful people of all walks of life to discuss different areas of business and life. I always ask them to tell a little bit of their story. The purpose of this is to illustrate in real life that the vast majority of people that have obtained success had two primary things in common. Most came from virtually nothing or had to overcome big obstacles and most have an attitude that they are going to succeed no matter what. They have faith in themselves that they can achieve their dreams. They have built in their minds that the only limiting factor on them is the limitations they put on themselves. It isn't because they are white or black, short or tall, handsome (like me) or ugly (like my brother). It is faith in themselves. This internal attitude is what they focus on as opposed to how they feel in the moment. Faith isn't denying there is a problem or obstacle, it is having the confidence or willingness to change to overcome the issue. Put another way: you drown, not by falling in the water, but by staying submerged in it!!!

My incredible business coach, Clay Clark, teaches that it is "Not about how you feel, it is about work – don't let your emotion get in the way of your motion!" I am not saying that successful people are always happy and always have a positive attitude. Anyone like that is either lying or insane. We all have self-doubt and get down at times and it is ok to get frustrated and want to quit. Yell, cuss, or kick the dog (figuratively!), but CHOOSE to change and push through. People too often let feelings determine their decisions instead of making decisions despite their feelings. Horst Schultz, co starter of Ritz Carlton told me on a phone interview that "I would rather make the decision about what I feel rather than letting my feelings decide who I am. Create excellence in everything. Excellence is a decision."

I have always said "I am a competitive guy by nature." One day when I said these words, I thought what does that really mean? Was I born competitive? Did nature make me competitive? Obviously the answer to both questions is no. I became competitive over periods of time by choosing to fight, to get up, and to not make excuses. These are areas of my life where I was forced to choose between fight or flee when faced with getting beat up by bigger kids or trying to protect my mom from abuse. I became competitive and developed an attitude that I will win or die trying. From a thousand choices being thrust upon me beyond my control, the only thing I could control was how I reacted. At this stage in my life, I feel bad for other people that have not had to struggle like I have. I see all my past now as a blessing that forced me to have the attitude I have today. Understand this... It is not your circumstances that determine your attitude! It is how you choose to react to your circumstances.

Michael Levine also said your winning attitude is "Born or created after a militant need to face the brutal facts that the game is not easy, the game is not fair, but the game is winnable." Let's think on these words for a minute. He says attitude is created after realizing life is not easy, not fair but winnable. Create an obsession to change, to grow, to adapt and to win. You can change your mind and thoughts which change the fruits of your labor. Do not let how you think stop your success because you literally and figuratively are the only excuse for not being successful!

Levine is one of my favorite speakers we have ever hosted at the workshops and at my home. He is brutally honest and says things like "Lazy is in direct correlation with entitlement." So lets talk about an entitlement attitude for a bit. In the world I live in today there is a huge segment of society that believes they are owed something. Maybe because of the color of their skin, the fact they grew up in a bad neighborhood, or their parents were alcoholics or abusive or... or ...or. One of the main reasons I decided to write this book is because I think this attitude is disgusting and extremely self-defeating. There have been riots I have witnessed in poor neighborhoods where the residents of those neighborhoods break into stores and loot, steal, burn and destroy. They think they are entitled to act in a certain way because of their circumstances. They destroy the businesses and lively hoods of people that live down the street from them; either not being aware or not caring that they are not only hurting the business owners they are destroying their own futures. They are destroying their ability to have stores and flourishing industry and leaving marks for years to come to prohibit other business minded people to invest in their communities. There is even a city right now in our great country that has said they will allow a poverty defense as an argument or excuse to not be punished for committing crime. I pray that if nothing else comes out of you reading this book, you understand that allowing bad behavior, or even worse, using a person's circumstances or past to justify such behavior, is only reinforcing the bad behavior.

The absolute worst thing you can do is lower the bar for measuring success or holding people accountable for bad choices based upon a person's race or circumstances. Imagine you have two kids. To one you say I expect you to get A's and B's and to the other you say I expect you to get C's and D's. You punish child one for getting a C but reward child two for getting a C. Which child have you hurt the most? I say child two because you planted in his mind that the expectation for him is subpar and shown him that the expectation for his sibling is higher, therefore making him think the other sibling must be smarter. Why else would the measuring stick be so different? Levine said, "If you want to be broke in American have a victim mentality." When we lower the bar of accountability, we create a mindset of being a victim.

This attitude that you are in charge of, also needs to be protected from outside influences. The things you hear from other people, TV, or music is the fertilizer for the seeds planted in your mind. You can plant a great garden but have it destroyed by weeds planted by other people. I heard a story early in my life that if you catch one crab from the sea and put it in a basket you have to put a lid on the basket or it will climb out. But if you have two or more in the basket you can take the lid off because one of the others will reach up and pull it back down when one tries to climb out. Your friends and family, often without realizing it, will be like those crabs. Every time you try to climb out of the basket of poverty or lack of success they reach up and pull you down with their words. You can't be successful. Our family has always been broke. Why do you think you are better than us. You cannot succeed because of the color of your skin. The deck is stacked against our race, our gender, our family, etc.! You have got to guard your mind from the poison of their words. You naturally think they know you better maybe then you know yourself. I am telling you that I know your potential better than they do and probably better than you do! Stop buying into their garbage. You get to choose your level of success. The best thing you can do for the poor is not be one! Levine says, "Fire your flakey friends because nothing will interfere with your capacity to reach your fullest potential like second hand fumes of their flakiness." Protect your mind like you would your home from an intruder because it is what is stolen from your mind that diminishes your potential. Your mind is more valuable than tangible belongings in your home! Follow Michael Levine's advice and tell anyone tearing you down "Your pathetic mediocrity is tainting my excellence". The great football coach Vince Lombardi once said, "We would accomplish more great things if we stopped thinking things were impossible".

STEP #2: CHANGING YOUR THOUGHTS AND ATTITUDE IS THE MOST VITAL STEP TOWARD SUCCESS!

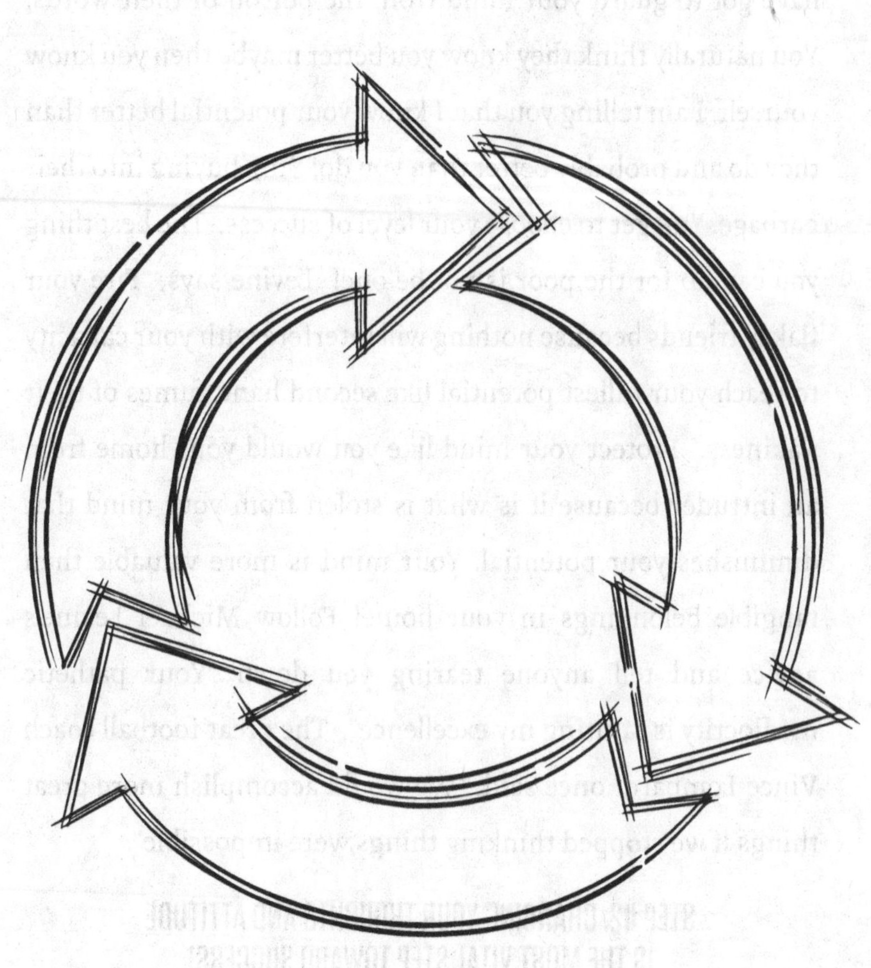

Chapter 3:

DEFINE, TAKE ACTION, MEASURE AND REFINE

"Do not wait: the time will never be
just right. Start where you stand,
and work with whatever tools you may
have at your command and better tools
will be found as you go along."
-Napoleon Hill

People that achieve success know no one is coming to save them so they have to take action to take care of themselves. I learned this principle early in life and developed a sort of "I do not need anyone" attitude. Said another way... If it is to be, it is up to me. No one is going to pull you from poverty. No one is going to break the chains of generational curses that are self-imposed on you by the choices you make in your life. No one is going to change your paradigm of poverty thinking, alcoholism, subpar effort, or drifting through life blaming others for your lack of success. You are the only person to blame and the only person to make changes. If my mom would have just went along the path that the rest of her family had in the past and continue to do to this day, there is no way I would be writing this book. I more than likely would have followed the path of my lineage and been an abusive alcoholic.

Have you heard these names... Beethoven, Roosevelt, Lincoln, Helen Keller, Ulysses S. Grant, or Benjamin Franklin? Of course you have. They all have had major impacts on all our lives. Did you know Beethoven was deaf, Roosevelt had Polio, Keller was deaf and blind, Grant was an alcoholic, and Franklin dropped out of school when he was ten years old. So, do you seriously think you don't have the power and ability inside you for success? I have never met you and I know without a doubt you do!

Napoleon Hill, in Think and Grow Rich, said "Expect, plan and demand what you desire." I could write an entire book on those seven words. Expect that you will be successful. Plan to achieve that success. Demand (never ever quit) until you achieve what you desire (define your dreams or goals). A few years ago my oldest son came to me and said, "Hey dad let's do this body building show." I was in decent shape and have always lifted weights but not even close to doing any type of show. I mean I didn't have a "dad bod" but was not lean and cut enough to even consider competing. The first thought that came to my mind was at fifty years old there is no way I am getting on stage in a speedo type bathing suit. Bryce explained to me that in physique competitions you wear normal thigh length men's suits.

We sought out a trainer to use and at our first meeting he measured and weighed us, discussed what work outs we were currently doing, and asked what our ultimate goals were. At our second meeting he laid out a very detailed plan of daily workouts and meal plan that we immediately started implementing. On Sunday nights I would spend a couple hours preparing my meals for the upcoming week. I knew exactly what I was going to eat ahead of time except for one meal a week was a cheat meal that I looked forward to with great anticipation. My workout was preplanned as well. I knew what movements and workouts I was going to do every day of the week, knew where I was going to do these workouts, had the time allotted in advance and what equipment and gear I would need. My trainer was in contact with me weekly to report to him what I had done the previous week, how much I weighed and if there were any issues I was having. As I progressed he periodically would modify the workout and my meal plan to keep me on pace.

At the end of sixteen weeks the day of the competition arrived. I had gone from 175 pounds to 147 (which is less that I weighed in high school) and if I do say so myself looked very sexy, from the neck down of course! At the end of the show, I found myself standing on stage holding a third place trophy at the age of fifty against a bunch of thirty five and above men. YAY ME right? No!!!! The only thing I did was be INTENTIONAL and stick to the plan! I literally only worked out fifteen minutes more a day that I was already doing but every movement had a purpose. Everything that went into my body had a purpose including the time of day. At 10:00 every morning I had to have eleven almonds. I don't know why it wasn't eight or fourteen almonds or some other number. My trainer, based upon his experience, dictated the plan and the results were predictable. The success I attained could be done by anyone that is willing to be INTENTIONAL and follow a plan. On our shirts for the competition, I had printed "success is being intentional". Did you know the average person watches six hours of television daily and is on their smart phone five hours a day? The opposite of being intentional is drifting.

This competition confirmed that success in everything can be predictable. If it is predictable, it can be duplicated by anyone regardless of who they are, where they come from, who their family is, or the color of their skin.

SUCCESS IS ACHIEVED WHEN YOU:

1. Define where you are right now;

2. Define where you want to go;

3. Create a plan to get there;

4. Measure the results of executing your plan;

5. Modify the plan to keep you on track to reaching your goal.

My trainer measured where I was by weighing me, measuring the size of different parts of my body, and inquiring about my current workout routine. He then helped me set a goal for where I wanted to be based upon how I wanted to perform in the competition. Through his experience, he created a plan of what to do and when to do it. Along the way he held me accountable, measured my progress against where I needed to be to hit my goal on time and modified the plan, adjusting based upon if I was ahead or behind schedule. Often we do not know even how to take ourselves through a process of success and must rely on other's experiences to guide us. You might notice how often I quote books. The vast knowledge contained for extremely low cost in books is a huge key to achieving success. Books can be your coach. The more you read the more you can achieve!

This success pattern applies whether your goal is physical, relational, or financial. The time it takes a particular individual to succeed in any thing is not the same as someone else but the fact that anyone can achieve success is the same. The time between where you are right now and where you want to go varies compared to other people's path, but the end result is anyone can succeed if they just persist.

DEFINE WHERE YOU ARE

First you have to define in detail where you are right now. Where is your money going, how are you developing your top asset (you), what is your lifestyle versus your income, how are you hiring people if you own a business? What advisors have you surrounded yourself with? What are you saying to yourself in your mind or self-talk, how are you spending your time, who are you spending your time with, what books are you reading or do you spend your time listening to radio or music? What are your strengths that you can capitalize on, what are your weaknesses that you need to work on, what limitations are you placing upon yourself, etc.? Self-evaluation requires tough love on yourself and potentially from others.

Evaluate everything you currently do and everything you spend time and money on. A good place to start financially is to gather twelve months worth of bank statements and credit card statements. Group all your expenses into categories like eating out, entertainment, gas, utilities, etc. Where you spend your money will say a lot about you including what your priorities are. Look for waste like reoccurring charges for things you don't use. Prioritize items from necessary to luxury to be able to direct where your money goes.

Even more important, detail every activity and action you take for a month or two. What is your daily schedule from the point you wake up to when you close your eyes? Carry a note pad or recorder with you to document your thoughts, what you watch, how you speak, who you are with and the positive or negative influence they have on you. Document what you do in your down time, what TV shows do you watch, what is playing in your car when you are driving. Be so detailed as to write down how many times you look at your phone, what you are looking at on your phone, who you are communicating with on your phone and what subjects are being discussed. This may all sound silly but you have got to paint as detailed a picture of your current situation as possible. Everything you do, hear, speak, and see plays a role in the choices you make daily, often unconsciously, which creates results. If you do not like or want to change your results you have to change the choices you make. Forgive me, but if you are not willing to do the detail work to change, you actually are choosing to not change. Do not blame others or where you come from or anything else. Your current condition has been chosen by YOU. If you want different do different. To do different you have to know where you are and why you make the choices you do.

DEFINE WHERE YOU WANT TO GO

Second, where do you want to be in ten years, five years, three years, one year, next month? I intentionally put long range before short range goals because you need to start with the end in mind then back into where you need to be in the short term to reach the long term. When you are setting goals, you should do so in all areas of your life including your faith, family, friends, fitness, fun and finances. My business coach, Clay Clark, calls those your F6 goals and teaches it is a necessity to a balanced happy life. Most people spend more time planning their vacation than their life. I am sure you have heard if you don't know where you are going, how will you ever know if you get there. Be very specific and push your limits of belief. Do not let your current belief system limit the heights of where you think you can go. In 2020 my accounting practice had a gross collection of just over five million dollars. My goal for my firm is to be at fifty million dollars in 60 months. That is a ten-fold growth and to be honest, I struggle to believe I will achieve it.

The reason I struggle is I am looking to the future through the eyes of my current situation. You should "shoot for the moon because if you miss you will land on top of the mountain". Most people don't set goals and if they do, they are safe goals. We fear failure, commitment, and disappointment. Most people embrace failure over striving for greatness because they live a life of making excuses.

The goals you set have got to be specific. Saying you want to be rich means nothing. What does being rich mean? How about I want to make one million dollars a year by the time I am fifty years old? That statement creates a detailed target with a detailed timeline. I can then break down that long range goal into mid-range and short-term goals. For instance, if you are thirty now and want to make a million a year in twenty years, how much should we target to be making at forty and thirty-five? You can have lofty goals and prove to yourself they are attainable by bringing them forward to short-term steps. If you are shooting a rifle at a target two miles away and you get off even by a tiny bit you will miss the target. If you bring that target to one hundred feet away and get off a little bit you will hit the target and be able to adjust.

CREATE A PLAN AND EXECUTE

Third, create a plan to get where you want to go. This is where the meat of success occurs. This is where you take what you have learned about yourself and where you want to go and make things actionable. Thomas Edison once said, "Vision without execution is hallucination". All the best laid goals and dreams are worthless without creating a specific plan and executing. Most of the time, this is the hardest part because your best thoughts and choices have gotten you to where you are right now. We all need coaches or counselors in our life. The greatest athletes in the world still have a coach. A coach has achieved success and learned steps to take to make the results of actions predictable. For most of my life, I have had to learn through the school of hard knocks. Trial and error as they say. If I was ever fortunate enough to be around anyone successful, I wanted to know how they achieved what they did. You can either learn from trying, failing, and trying again or you can acquire the knowledge you need from other's failures and successes. The knowledge you seek is often cheap or free. You have got to be a reader to be successful. The knowledge and experiences that others have taken the time to document is more valuable than any college degree. We live in a country that teaches people to go to college to learn to be a technician, taught by people that normally have not achieved any level of success in the subjects they are teaching. Living in the United States of America provides us all with the greatest opportunity to be successful ever known to man. The problem is we generally do not teach our system of economics. We do not teach people how to create wealth by leveraging time, people, and money. We teach people to be a good technician. A good doctor, plumber or accountant, trading hours for dollars thereby limiting the amount of money we can make. Zig Ziglar said "If your money is contingent upon showing up you have a problem." At the end of this book, I will list books that have played a huge role in my life. These books were the key to my success.

I spent most of my professional life working my tail off to achieve success. As of December 2020, I have acquired twenty-three accounting practices that total approximately ten million in revenue. In 2020 we collected just over five million. I literally paid ten million dollars and have retained half that much. I just busted down every wall that got in my way to "throw as much mud on the wall" as possible to see what would stick. I had no plan but to just do MORE. I remember my junior year in high school people talking about going to college. I seriously had no idea of what college was. I had good grades but thought nothing about what was next. I decided to go to a small school in Oklahoma because I thought I was good at football. After I got tired of getting beat on, I transferred to Oklahoma State University (the finest school in all of America) to finish a degree in accounting. I worked hard and continued to get good grades not thinking about what jobs would be available. Upon graduation I received multiple offers from eight of the largest accounting firms in the world, even though I knew nothing of their existence until I started interviewing. For most of my life, I was just in a pack of people that was moving forward not knowing where we were going but working hard at whatever I was asked to do. I was drifting and not being intentional, except I intentionally worked hard. I guess the lesson here is if you are going to follow a crowd be sure the crowd is moving forward toward success and then outwork everyone in the crowd until you open your eyes and see you can lead the crowd.

During that period of my life, I was running away from a life more than running toward a dream. The choices my mom made to separate us from the generational bad decisions of both sides of my family allowed me to see a life I did not want. We were poor, on food stamps, and government assistance for a good part of my youth but we had a place to sleep and basic needs were met. My mom worked multiple jobs and showed me that hard work created choices that my cousins did not have. I used to love to go see my cousins and be rowdy. All kinds of fun; stealing things, getting into fights, smoking pot and drinking.

As I grew older and watched my mom's hard work to put me into different schools with kids that didn't do that kind of stuff, I started disliking the things I did with my cousins. I saw that what I thought was normal behavior was not. I owe it to my mom for getting me into the middle of a crowd of people that were moving in a different direction.

I continued my "go with the flow but work harder than anyone else" drifting until I started my own business in 1992. At the age of 25 I was married, and with two infant sons I bought the local accounting office that I was working for but it did not provide enough for us to pay our bills. For the first time in my life, I had to think forward. No one was taking care of me, no paycheck, no mom, no college scholarships, no food stamps, and no government entitlements. All the sudden, I had three people that were looking to me to provide for them based upon no guaranteed paycheck. I took a full-time job at a local manufacturing company making real good money and planned on working my accounting practice on the side. I thought life was good. Two weeks into my new job I thought I was going to die emotionally. It was really a good job, but I found out very quickly that I was not someone who could work in corporate America. It was boring and lacked the potential I knew I wanted but didn't know how to get. I started calling other accounting practices in my hometown desperate to increase the size of my side business to a point it would support my family. Once again, I found myself running away from something I didn't want instead of running toward something I wanted. A little secret I can share with you, most of the time running from something are a much greater motivator than running towards something. The bad you have in your life is real and tangible and immediate. The good you want in the distant, is intangible and much easier to give up on. Count yourself lucky if you weren't born with a silver spoon in your mouth because your chances for ultra-success is much greater. The strength you generate from the pain you suffer and the motivation to work towards something greater is immense. Those of us that grew up poor have to fight victim mentality while those that are "luckier" in life have to fight complacency.

One of the best books I have ever read is The Subtle Art of Not Giving a F*ck by Mark Manson. The language is horrible but the message is life changing. Mark says "You don't have to have inspiration or motivation to take action. Start with action no matter how small to create inspiration and motivation." So many people think that they have to be inspired to create motivation that creates action. The reality is successful people are generally just people that do not let lack of motivation stand in their way of action. People often look for any excuse not to have to do the daily boring things that success commands. A few years ago, I was getting out of my car at my office and a car parked next to me. On the rear window of this car was a 26.2 sticker on one side and a 0.0 sticker on the other. My curiosity got the best of me, so I asked the owner of the car what they meant. She proudly told me that the 26.2 meant she ran a marathon and the 0.0 meant her husband has not ran anything! Know this, I was a football player, and my limit was running one hundred yards. I hated long distance running but I was stuck. I had to have a 26.2 sticker! I told friends and family I was going to run a marathon and heard virtually zero encouragement. Words like are you stupid, that is idiotic, and why would you do something like that were repeated to me. I had no answer other than I had to have a 26.2 sticker. It took me almost two years of training be comfortable with being able to complete the run. I worked my way up through 5ks, 15k, then a half marathon. Finally, I signed up for a full marathon four months away and created a plan to train. I sought the advice of others who had ran before, got the appropriate shoes for the style of my stride and started on a path, that I disliked, every single step. Seven days a week I argued with myself every morning hours before I normally would get up. "Just stop Paul, stay in bed Paul, it is freezing outside Paul, you're an idiot Paul, why are you doing this Paul, it is just a stupid sticker Paul". I had the very definition of lack of motivation or inspiration. I had no support or cheering from my friends or family, nor did

I seek it. It would have been "normal" to just stop and quit. I pulled myself out of bed kicking and screaming mentally like a little baby, day after day after day with the action of training without motivation.

Charles Colaw, who owns several multi-million-dollar gyms and is a friend and client of mine, said "The battle is won by making your feet hit the ground within five seconds of the alarm going off." My focus therefore was not on running hours and hours, it was setting the alarm at night and thinking five seconds Paul, five seconds. Once I was up then the table was turned and I would have had to reverse my path to fail that day. The action of hearing my alarm and my feet hitting the ground within five seconds created the motivation to complete my task of training for the day.

A little secret for you, often times when you push yourself and are on a path to victory things happen to try to derail you. Three weeks before the day of the marathon, I was out running on a cold winter morning on the back roads of rural Oklahoma and stepped on an object in the road as I moved to the edge to allow an oncoming car to not run me over. My ankle went completely sideways and swole up to three times normal size. I could barely walk and had not reached the pinnacle of the miles I needed to run in order to feel comfortable that I could complete the 26.2 mile task ahead of me. After having it x-rayed, my doctor came into the little room I had patiently been waiting in and told me it was cracked but not broken and that if I could stand the pain, I could wear an air cast and run in three weeks. I had the perfect excuse to quit. No one would have blamed me or called me a quitter, but I would have.

I had sacrificed so much to that point that there was no way I wasn't going to run and get my sticker. I had bought my pink running cold gear shirt, pink socks and black and pink shorts and had told my mom who had Breast Cancer I was running for her. I had endured cold, rain, snow, lack of sleep, hours upon hours away from home. I had trained complaining to myself constantly fighting the urge to quit and just roll over. You see, it was no longer about the sticker. My ACTION had created MOTIVATION and had turned into INSPIRATION.

I forced myself to have a no-quit, no-surrender attitude by putting simple action before the slightest motivation or inspiration existed. I would not quit or fail. At the twenty-mile mark, I didn't think I could go on. I was angry that I had put myself in this situation, exhausted to the point of collapse, I had been running in a crowd of thousands of people not one of which I knew. I had just been passed by a woman who had to be in her eighties when I rounded a corner and saw a woman that reminded me of my mom. I thought of her never quit attitude, unselfish love and sacrifice for me, and my anger and frustration turned instantly into unstoppable tears. I was a grown man crying like a baby with uncontrollable emotion driven by pain, exhaustion, and a desire to succeed and not disappoint. With renewed energy to not quit, I finished the 26.2 mile run and limped across the finish line. The race was the most difficult thing I have ever done. I literally could not step down off the curb on the way to my car. I was mentally, physically, and emotionally exhausted but the joy and pride inside me had never been higher. Putting ACTION ahead of MOTIVATION and INSPIRATION turned a quest to get a stupid sticker into a victory that taught me I can achieve anything. Simply being willing to act even when I didn't want to, changed my life.

MEASURE YOUR PROGRESS

Fourth, have a way to measure the progress of implementing your plan. For the third time, we measure what we treasure. This is true in every aspect of life. We all are accustom to measuring things. How often do you look at the gas gauge in your car, check the weather to decide what to wear, step on that communist lying device in your bathroom that tells you how much you weigh? You have to measure the more important things in your life as well. Imagine if you go to the doctor not feeling well and the nurse does not take your vital signs. When the doctor comes in, she says well your blood pressure, heart rate, and lungs looked great six months ago! The value of those measurements from six months ago have as much value as you evaluating your financial position, tax status, budget, or personal growth plan looking backwards. Most people do not know even how to measure or even what to measure. Seek the help of a coach or professional to help establish what are called key performance indicators (KPIs) for you personally and for your business if applicable.

KPIs are simply things that you can measure in the short term to determine if you are on track to hit your long-term goals. As discussed earlier my current goal is to be a fifty-million-dollar accounting firm by the end of 2025. That is a huge goal of almost ten times growth. How do I measure if I am on track? Where do I need to be in three years to hit that goal? In two years? One year? In ninety days? The key to success is what do I need to accomplish this week to create a growth curve to hit my target in five years. In training for the body building contest, I knew I needed to lose one and a half pounds a week to reach the desired weight in sixteen weeks. If I focused on loosing twenty-eight pounds it would have been overwhelming. I had not been down to 147 pounds since I was fifteen years old. My mind would not have been able to believe I could do it. I could however focus on losing one and a half pounds this week.

I have broken down my path to reaching fifty million dollars in gross collections in sixty months to interim goals of twelve million in one year, nineteen million in two, twenty-seven in three, and thirty-seven in four. To hit those goals, through my experience of success and failure and through evaluating past performance as well as seeking the guidance of my advisors and team, I know I have to call three accounting practices a week to try to acquire them, get five google reviews a week, and bring in seven new clients a week. My KPIs are these weekly numbers. My focus is on these short-term attainable goals. As I proceed week to week, month to month, I can plot my growth course numerically to see if I am still on track to hit the next goal. If I am not, then I increase the activity.

In addition to these financial growth driven measurables, I also know that I will outgrow my own abilities and therefore have to change and grow me. I know that the person I am today cannot run nor manage a business ten times my current size. I therefore know I need to read two new books a month, I need to meet with my coach weekly. I need to identify others that have accomplished similar goals and seek their advice on obstacles. I need to constantly be on the search to hire new and better team members even if I do not need them today. I need to continually review my cash flow and available working capital or access to cash from borrowing, etc.

An extremely important thing to remember regardless of where you are in life is "You do not know what you do not know!" Chart out your progress of where you need to be and where you are currently. If I only lost half a pound in a week, I knew I was behind and had to do more the next week to make up. Know your numbers! Convert goals into short term measurable numbers and fixate on them. Be maniacal and obsessed about hitting them. So many people have dreams and vision as to where they want to go or be in life. People that achieve those goals are hard-headed, action driven people. They do not accept no for an answer and refuse to quit.

To be productive start with the end in mind, but activity is getting things done. Creating a measurable short-term plan allows you to know exactly what activity you need to be doing today to keep marching towards success. Measuring is a vital part of being successful and is most often the thing that people omit because it is boring and requires real attention to the detail effort instead of just dreaming. Understand however, that nothing matters without action. If you take the time to establish a budget which includes five hundred dollars a month for eating out, just because you know it is the twenty-fifth of the month and you already spent your budget, if you still eat out all your measuring and planning is worthless. The success plan is define, take action, measure and refine. It is not define, measure, measure, measure and measure.

A majority of the successful people I know are "ready, fire, aim" people. Action can overcome a lack of measuring but all measuring and no action is futile. In war, to advance, a General normally has to expose his flanks. The founder of American's Naval forces, John Paul Jones, said "Those that will not risk cannot win." There is definitely luck involved in being successful, but it is normally simply recognizing opportunity and not procrastinating. In 2006 my wife, Lori, and I thought we had found our forever home after nineteen years of marriage. We had a five thousand square foot country French home on one hundred and sixty five acre ranch. We had cattle, horses and everything we had ever wanted or really dreamed of.

In 2017 my oldest son sent me a link to a 25,000 square foot house that a doctor had been building on for twelve years. He had gotten the house complete on the outside and ready to start the finishing touches on the inside with a total investment so far of approximately $6,200,000. Apparently, he had made some bad life decisions and had been trying to sell this property on eighty-nine acres for a few years. He was close to bankruptcy and had dropped the price to $4,900,000. Lori nor I had any interest in moving but from pure curiosity called the realtor and set a time to tour the home. I don't know how many 25,000 square foot homes you have been in, but I had been in exactly zero. When we rounded the wooded corner and first saw the house our reaction was holy sh*t! It was both overwhelming huge and absolutely gorgeous. It was a cold and rainy early winter evening and the home had no electricity. We had to use our cell phones as flashlights to tour the home and to our utter fear and amazement there were bats flying around inside. Imagine Bruce Wayne's mansion with the bats from his dark cave flying all around.

The home had a two-story theater room, a gym the size of most commercial gyms, seven stair cases, thirty-one exterior doors, and one hundred and nine interior doors. The pantry was the size of a normal apartment and had a staircase that led to the master bedroom so a person could go get a snack in their underwear at night. The master bedroom suite was two stories with seven closets, a massive craft room and grandkids bedroom attached. The master bathroom had a shower that was the size of our living room in our first apartment in college and had a toilet room with a bidet. At some point in my early childhood life, I saw a bidet on a movie and thought, " wow you know you have made it if you have one of those". A word of caution though, when checking a bidet out, don't lean over it to turn the water on as it will shoot you square in the face. The master suite itself was pretty close to the size of our current home.

There were three kitchens, three laundry rooms (including one in the master suite), thirteen bathrooms, seven fireplaces and a six-story tower with a balcony on four sides right in the middle of the house. It literally took us over an hour to walk through the house. We had a great time looking and dreaming about the potential the home had but we had no need for such a large home and had no interest in paying close to five million for a house. The words "luck is simply recognizing opportunity and not procrastinating" kept coming to my mind.

As "luck" had it, I had just finished reading Never Split the Difference by Chris Voss. Mr. Voss was a former FBI hostage negotiator teaching me how to negotiate! For fun I tested out my newly acquired skills and proceeded to "set an extreme anchor" and offered $1,100,000 for this massive structure and the 89 acres it sat on. Oh, did I mention that it also had a 2,000 sq foot pool house and a massive airplane-hanger perfect for filling up with exotic cars! I assume the seller would be insulted and just reject my offer without even responding. To my amazement a day or so later I heard from the realtor with a counter offer of $1,900,000. They came down $3,000,000 and were willing to take $4,300,000 less than the owner had invested in the property. Mr. Voss also taught me to never stop with the first counteroffer. I ended up signing a contract to purchase the home for $1,500,000!!! At that time, I did not realize the easy part was signing the contract. I had no idea how difficult it would be to get a bank to loan $1,500,000 on a home appraised at over $6,000,000. Five different banks told me no. The common concern was something has to be wrong with the home because how could anyone get that good of a deal!

President Donald Trump in his book The Art of the Deal, said "Sheer persistence is often the difference between success and failure." If I possess any great skill, it is because I am extremely persistent. I am a man of faith and I fail God often, but I pray constantly. My prayer is always "God if you don't want me to walk through this door, please lock it, weld it shut, bolt it and make it impossible for me to break through." Both God and I know that I will beat my head on that door, look for alternate routes, and look for any way possible to make it happen if I am convinced that it is a good deal. I need God to make sure I do not get through that door!!! Persistence paid off as well as creative thinking. I went to the bank that currently held the non-performing loan on this mansion and begged, pleaded, threatened and sweet talked them into making me a loan to purchase with additional funds to finish the construction. This was the first time in the history of this bank they had ever loaned more money on a non-performing property.

The comical thing is the number of builders that were absolutely livid when they heard about the deal I negotiated. I have always had the philosophy that the answers is always no to the questions you do not ask. Success follows those that take action. I say again "Luck is having an opportunity and acting instead of procrastinating." You can only be successful at things you are willing to fail trying to get. Fear of failure inhibits success and actually leads to failure. We all fail but successful people face those failures and keep pushing. Take action, face the no's and push through to get the pretty girl, find a way to close the deal, and make your competition mad. "When things are bad, eat the weak, and grow your business", Tilman Fertitta in Shut Up And Listen.

STEP #3: DEFINE WHERE YOU ARE AND WHERE YOU WANT TO GO, CREATE A PLAN TO GET THERE, AND MEASURE THE RESULTS AS YOU GO TO ALLOW YOU TO REFINE YOUR PLAN!

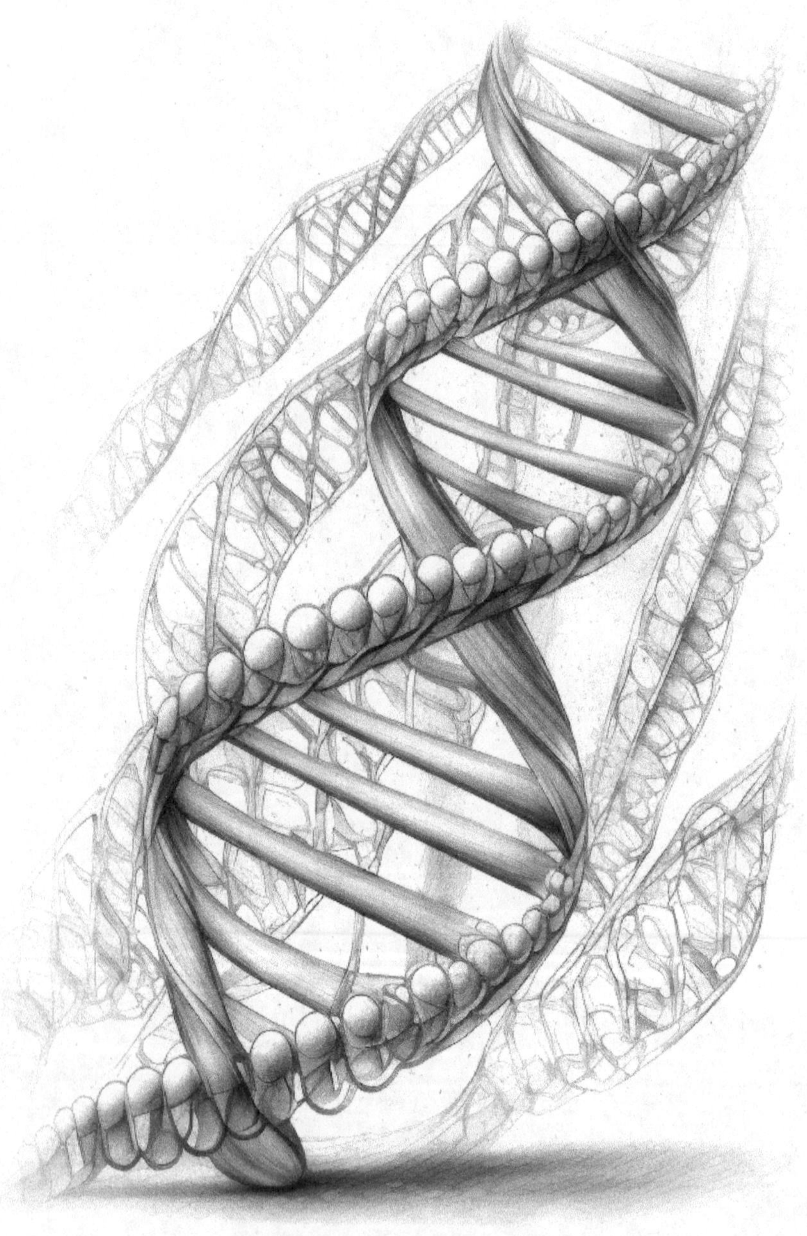

Chapter 4:

ONCE YOU GET IT RIGHT, CLONE YOURSELF

"Once you nail it, Scale it!"
-Dr. Robert Zoellner

I am asked to speak frequently about success principles, and I fear that most people miss the opportunity to be ultra-successful because the principles I talk about are too simple. They hear them but often do not apply them thinking there has to be some sort or top-secret formula instead. I will make a very bold statement here "If you have not achieved success, you either have not learned the laws of success or have not put them into operation." Napoleon Hill's book Think and Grow Rich is seen by many as the top success principle book ever written. His 20 years spent interviewing the most successful people of his time for the common denominator for success came down to "Definiteness of purpose and unwavering desire." His synopsis both makes me angry and excites me. He did not say these successful people had an amazing product or service, spoke with eloquence above the rest of us, or had a once-in-a-lifetime lucky break, that didn't have any type of amazing talent or any other common personal characteristic except that they focused on what they wanted, refused to quit, and had designed their activities to intentionally achieve their goals.

Whether you are an employee or a business owner, you cannot create wealth on your own. You have to leverage time, people and money. You have to figure sh*t out then clone yourself by breaking down how you do things so other less skilled people can do a large portion of what you do. The staff that works for me become more valuable to my organization by taking work off me and anyone that is between me and them or by finding ways to automate processes to make things run simpler, and with less effort. The next few paragraphs apply to my business but also apply to you in any position you have.

After twenty-five years of owing my own business, I had grown from nothing to $2,000,000 in gross collections. The average CPA that owns his own practice caps out at about $600,000. We were above-average but my business still was contingent upon me showing up. I was trading hours for dollars like 99% of Americans. I knew there had to be a better way. I wanted to go from successful to systematic! I tried to buy or even "borrow" an operations manual from a national firm. True wealth comes from creating income sources that continue on without your active involvement. I wanted to get paid even if I didn't show up! What I was craving is a methodology to scale my business. My good friend Dr. Robert Zoellner says "once you nail it, you scale it." Compared to the average one owner public accounting firm, I had nailed it but with my current model it was impossible to go further. Simply put, I needed to duplicate myself. Most accounting firms accomplish this by bringing in partners that build the business bigger by sharing expenses. I did not want to grow my business by sharing the fruits with other owners thereby limiting my ability to create wealth. Partners would allow me to increase my income some but was not an answer to creating wealth. Instead, I wanted to share the fruits of success with the staff that helped me build it through incentives and rewarding extra effort and results.

In 2018 I was introduced to a business coach named Clay Clark. Mr. Clark was nothing like I expected, or thought would benefit me. I came from a professional work environment and was thrown back a little when I met him. He was younger than me, looked like a white rapper and was as much a comedian as a businessperson. Clay and I embarked upon a journey of "uneducating" me about a lot of the complex business ideas I had learned in college and working for other CPAs. He made statements like "Simplicity scales, complexity fails", "Don't let your emotion get in the way of your motion", and "For success there is no hocus pocus only maniacal focus." I did not understand what any of that had to do with running a CPA business. Surely if these types of statements were the keys to being successful, I would have learned them in college or heard my bosses say similar things. Over the next three years, I learned the key to scaling any business, even a wisdom-based business such as mine, is creating simple, repeatable processes.

He taught me that every minute I spent being a technician my business was not growing. Instead of doing CPA tasks like tax returns or accounting, as the leader of my firm, I needed to be training, planning, documenting, growing, and measuring. I was trained to be a CPA and do CPA stuff but learned to be extra successful, I should not be doing CPA stuff!!!! That did not make sense to me. As we walked this path, it hit me that I had done CPA stuff very well for a long time but had plateaued because there was only so much time for me to overachieve at being a CPA. As Dr. Zoellner says, I had nailed it but now I had to scale it! I had to take a complex wisdom-based business and simplify it to a point that I could grow it without partners. Basically, I had to take nearly 30 years of knowledge and operations centered around me as the driver and "dumb it down" so I was less important to my company to allow growth beyond me.

The basic tools of scaling any business or position in a business are using documented processes, breaking jobs into tasks, checklists for all important steps, software to automate as much as possible and being proactive and not reactive with time management. My business stopped growing because most of the secrets were tied up in my mind.

DOCUMENT EVERYTHING YOU DO

Whether you understand it or not you have processes for doing things. We all do in every aspect of our lives. For instance, think about how you put your socks and shoes on. I bet you do it the same way every time. Do you put on one sock then a shoe then the other sock and shoe, do you put both socks on then shoes, do you start with your left foot or right? We are creatures of habit in both our personal life and financial life. This principle is why one of the keys to success is creating correct habits to repeat, like saving before you spend, reading personal growth books to grow YOU, living by a budget, and for God's sake putting both socks on then your shoes! Get to the very basics of what you do and how you do it. Carry a note pad around for a month or two to document what you do every day and exactly how you do it. What tools do you use? What words do you use? What steps are involved? Document with as much detail as possible. Strive to leave not even the simplest of steps out. Do not assume others will know what you are talking about or know that you left out any steps. Assume that someone that has no technical knowledge will need to understand what you are doing and how you are doing it.

Among other great dishes, my wife makes an amazing lasagna. My grown kids and their wives have a lot of frustration when they try to replicate her dishes because her recipes are full of "grandmas" steps that she learned over her lifetime. I think it may be on purpose, but very few of her meals can be replicated based upon any documentation available. Your success pattern (way of doing things) or business is full of "recipes" for success. You cannot expect others to replicate your success with vague documentation. All this assumes you are good at what you do. You can and should use these documenting steps to evaluate how you do things and ask, "Are there better ways to doing things?" If you have a team or have surrounded yourself with qualified advisors, they can and will take your "recipes" and improve on them.

BREAK YOUR JOB OR JOBS IN YOUR COMPANY INTO TASKS

Most business owners or key employees have figured out how to get things done in such a way that they tend to be the best at what they do. There is nothing wrong necessarily with being the best in your organization at what you do except that there is only one you. Until they invent a way to clone you, you have to figure out how to duplicate yourself. You can either use the old methods of having an apprentice and take years for you the "master" to teach someone what to do, or teach many people to do parts of what you do. It is much easier to teach ten people to be able to do ten parts of what makes you successful versus finding one person to be able to master all ten steps.

The steps to do a tax return at my office including the following:

- Initial meeting to gather data and ask questions;

- Scan client data to our electronic file cabinet;

- Set up project in our tracking system;

- Data entry person enters basic data;

- Tax preparer enters remainder of data;

- Tax reviewer checks return for errors and issues;

- Print and Invoice return;

- Contact client for delivery; and

- Transmit return to tax authority.

When I first started my business, I literally did every single step. We currently do over 9,000 tax returns. Do you think I could do a tenth of those returns if I did every step? Not possible! Take what you do and focus on being the tip of the sword. What is it that you do to be successful? By breaking your "job" as an owner or employee into the individual steps and documenting how you do those steps you create a "play book" for what has made you successful. Merge exactly what you say and what you do into the individual tasks of your success pattern to have a documented process to teach others and to free up your time to do what you do best. By doing this, you have not cloned yourself but have cloned what you do. The exciting thing that happens is you will find people that will improve how you did individual tasks thereby making your success pattern even stronger!!!!

USE CHECKLISTS, SOFTWARE, AND THE LOWEST SKILLED PEOPLE

The basis for the saying "Simplicity scales and complexity fails," lies in who or what can do the steps in a process that makes up an activity. If a task is complex, it necessitates skill or abstract thought to duplicate. Creating duplicity and scalability requires making things so simple that someone with little skill could follow a checklist to execute the task or the task could be accomplished with less skilled people through the use of software. When I say less skilled it is not an insult but being able to hire less skilled people will solve a big problem that most businesses have in hiring "good people."

Look at every task of a job and how you have documented to do it, then create a step by step "how to" list. Have a checklist for opening the business, for closing, for answering the phone, making an appointment, dealing with unhappy customers, and every other step that it takes to be successful. Make is so easy that an employee doesn't have to think just execute. I am not discouraging the ability for your employees or people you supervise to give input and think outside the box to make things better. I am however saying that they do not deviate from your success model without YOU changing the predetermined steps.

HIRE PROACTIVELY BASED UPON ATTITUDE INSTEAD OF APTITUDE

Now that you have taken a job, broken it down into tasks, documented as simply as possible what you do and say, and created checklists, scripts and utilized software to push as much as possible to the least skilled person possible, how do you find "good people"? Without a doubt the number one statement I hear from managers and business owners is "I cannot find good people." The reality is there are tons and tons of good people just not good people with the skills to do the job at hand. We defeat that whole argument by doing the hard work of breaking a skilled job into tasks. Let me ask you a question.... Does a professional football team put ads on Indeed or other job searching sites when their starting quarterback gets hurt, look at resume's, set up 20 interviews to only have 10 people show up, then pick the best of the applicants that showed up? No, they already have his replacement ready to step in. So why do you as a manager or owner?

A professional sports team is always hiring and always looking to upgrade its players. This may be a tough pill for you to swallow but you should do the same. If you have a copy machine that works about half the time, do you go over and hug it and encourage it or do you replace it? I know, I know, we are dealing with people here and not a machine. You should give your employees or subordinates clear guidelines of what is expected and give them two maybe three chances to correct actions but beyond that they have to go. To have this attitude of always upgrading and expecting the best you cannot allow your people to hold you hostage because you need them too much.

My business is always looking for people with an attitude and desire to learn and be given an opportunity. You can teach skill to someone with desire, but you cannot teach desire to someone who has skill. Every now and then we find a rare diamond that has skill and desire. We use a group interview process on at least a monthly and sometimes weekly schedule regardless of whether we have a need to hire anyone. We place ads with specific language tailored toward attitude but also reference the possible positions we generally hire and request they contact us via email. We generally get 20 to 30 responses to which we reply thank you for your interest, we have a time open this day or another at 5:00 which works best for you? Of those that respond back with which day works best for them, we email great, see you then and please dress for success, bring a resume' and be on time.

The day of the interview we lock the door at 5:05 because this is a tryout for them. If they cannot be on time, they disqualify themselves. They can however come to another interview. If 20 people say they will be there generally about 12 show up. The sad thing is everyone thinks they are having a one-on-one interview. Literally almost half of the people do not show up! The entire interview process takes 30 to 45 minutes and begins with an introduction to our business, what we stand for and what our core values are. The individuals there are then asked to introduce themselves and tell why they are there, followed by us asking them three predetermined questions. We finish with giving them the opportunity to ask us any questions they have.

At this point we still HAVE NOT LOOKED AT THEIR RESUME!

We look at if they were on time, did they dress professionally, did they bring their resume with them? Can they follow those three simple directions? We look at how they communicate, do they have a good attitude, do they look us in the eye, do they have a personality that we like and would fit in with our team, and what question(s) did they ask. Understand that we do NOT need any of them! We flip the interviewing process on its head. When you need someone, you tend to settle for who you can get. When you do not need anyone, you can smile and send them all on their way. We dismiss them all and ask that they leave their resumes and the answer sheets and we will contact them if we want them to come back for the next step which is a formal interview and potentially shadowing one of our team members.

Skill in the area we are looking for is a bonus but not the most important requirement. The process of doing group interviews saves us time and puts us in the driver's seat in the hiring game. If our goal is to create wealth through leveraging people, we must base our success on the success of others. The better the people you surround yourself with the easier it is to help them be successful, and thus the quicker it is for you to "clone" yourself by teaching them the skill to do tasks that you have documented as a part of what you do to be successful.

Always, always be looking to hire and upgrade your team! If you can't find good people, it is your fault because they are out there. You probably have not documented the required tasks to a level that allows less skilled people to succeed. The final and probably the most important step to "cloning" you is to have a daily meeting with your people. My business coach told me this for almost two years until I actually put it into action. I missed the point that a daily meeting with your team is the primary key to scaling and transferring experience and wisdom. At this daily meeting your team members ask questions and by answering their question you are educating your entire team. The team grows and expands to be able to accomplish higher and higher tasks that you used to be the only one able to do, freeing you up to continue to grow and buy back your time. The more advanced your team gets the more they add to their own success and thus your success.

Once you get buy in from your team and they become more confident the door opens to the creation of incentive based pay structures. When you put in the hands of your team the ability to increase their pay through extra effort and performance, you change their mentality from and employee to an owner. They now can produce and receive additional rewards because you design plans to tie extra income to extra results. The net result is they produce more and earn more but SO DO YOU!!

BE PROACTIVE AND NOT REACTIVE WITH YOUR TIME

Concentration is a muscle in that the more you exercise it the better it gets and the more interruptions the weaker it gets. Aubrey Marcus says in his book Own the Day, "Research shows the average person responds to emails in 6 seconds and takes 64 seconds to return to the task they were performing." We all have 24 hours in a day, no more no less. The good and bad news is you get to choose how you use those hours. Do you sleep 10 hours or 6? Do you get up early or sleep in? Do you listen to rap music or a book? Do you watch 6 hours of tv a day like the "average person" or watch podcasts to learn? Be proactive not reactive with your time. This path toward success hinges on your personality, skills, and aptitude. You are the tool that will determine your success or lack thereof. Grow you and your life will change. Be very intentional with your time because you will blink and 5 years will go by.

The specific areas that you will need to address in controlling your time are maintaining a single calendar, controlling "gotta minute" meetings, and preplanning your day with to-do lists. Schedule EVERYTHING in your calendar. Every aspect of your personal and professional life needs to be on your calendar. I know it sounds silly but if you are taking your spouse out on a date put it on the calendar (if you don't have a date scheduled, for God's sake and for your safety get one scheduled!!). Schedule when you will have family time, time to exercise, time to read and reflect, time when you will check emails, time for fun, time to be on social media, time for bible study or meditation, time to do your accounting, and every other thing that is important and must get done. If you don't schedule it, it probably will not get done. Avoid the effect of losing time by preplanning what is important and when it will get done. Anyone that has played football or other sports at a high level knows that successful teams do not just show up to practice and figure it out as they go. The day is planned down to the minute to enable them to accomplish as much as possible during the available time. Time for stretching, agilities, blocking drills, receiver drills, quarterback drills, tackling, team offense, defense, special teams, and rest breaks are preplanned to the exact minute. When you are on a path to success you cannot waste a minute. People that do not preplan daily, weekly, monthly activities will drift and accomplish much less. In Outwitting the Devil, Napoleon Hill went so far as saying the best tool of the devil to get people to sin and be less than what God intended for them to be was to be unintentional and drift.

> "A man does not have the right to occupy another man's time," **John D Rockefeller**

As important as what you do with your time is, it's equally as important what you allow others to do with it. Have you ever had someone come up to you and say "gotta minute?" No one has the right to steal your time and you should protect your time because it is the most valuable thing you have. I made a rule that unless the building is on fire, or some other emergency is involved "I do not have a minute." Generally speaking, when someone wants to interrupt me, it can wait. I schedule one or two times per day on my calendar to allow my staff to come and discuss issues. The funny thing is by scheduling in these times, a majority of the things they "need" to discuss they figure out themselves which further proves that it would have been a waste of my time. In The Millionaire Map, Jim Stovall says "When you waste time you are not only standing still you are failing to move in the direction you should be traveling."

One of the first things or last things on your calendar should be 30 minutes to an hour to update your to-do list. Some people like to do it first thing in the morning which gets your proactive juices flowing, while others like to do it the last thing of the day so they can hit the next day running when their feet hit the ground. If you take an hour to plan you will get more accomplished in the remaining 7 hours (if you only work 8) than you would have in 10 hours. You maintain focus and as you complete tasks you already know what the next thing to do is. With your list in place, prioritize and execute. Determine the highest priority tasks and execute. Try to touch things once by either accomplishing the task or pushing it to someone else to do. Even the act of reading a to-do list multiple times is a waste of precious time.

Please don't make the mistake of underestimating the power of preplanning what you want to accomplish by using to-do lists. Success is very simple but not easy. Those that consistently utilize a to-do list understand the power of this simple success principle. When I first started using a to-do list, I allowed other people to put things that I needed to get accomplished on my list. It very quickly got out of control. I learned that it was just another way that other people were controlling my time instead of me. This is your day, so take responsibility for how you spend it and what you accomplish. Stay until you get the important things done. Refuse to push things forward unless you absolutely have to. Make today serve today and not steal from tomorrow!

No one has a crystal ball and the future is unpredictable, but an intentionally planned and executed life brings predictability. Dave Ramsey once said that whether a person lives in poverty or not can be predicted with a 70% probability based upon four life choices. His research shows that if a person graduates high school, gets a job, gets married after the age of 20, then has kids they have a 70% chance of not living in poverty. How simple and basic is that. Imagine if this was taught and adhered to, what it would do to the impoverished in this country. How many social problems would dramatically decrease if our youth would be at least intentional to the point of following this simple life plan? Success in all aspects of life is similarly simple but will you follow them, or will the path be so simple that you overlook it or skip steps?

Take control of your path to success by detailing where you are now and make specific and measurable goals for where you want to go. Create a plan with the help of a coach to reach your goals; measure the results of your actions to adjust your activities; document everything you do, break your "job" into tasks; use checklists and software to have the lowest skilled person complete tasks you formally did. Hire proactively based upon attitude then teach skill. Control your time with a level of intentionality that reflects how disastrous it is to waste. This paragraph on its own can make you a wealthy person if you build your financial life around it. What you do with it is up to you!

STEP #4: CLONE YOURSELF THROUGH THE USE OF DOCUMENTED PROCESSESS, HIRE PROACTIVELY FOR ATTITUDE INSTEAD OF SKILL, AND PROATIVELY CONTROL YOUR TIME.

Chapter 5:
SAVE BEFORE YOU SPEND

"If you don't have the ability to save you do
not have the seeds of greatness inside you"
-Brian Tracy

One of the best books I have ever read is The Richest Man in Babylon by George Clason. The fictional character lives in ancient Babylon and becomes a very wealthy man by following some very basic principles (isn't it strange how success principles always seem to be simple but require a diligent consistent effort). The primary principle is to save the first 10% of what you make and create a lifestyle on the remainder. I would go further and say you should give away or tithe the first 10% then save a minimum of the second 10% and live on the remainder. We will discuss later the principle of reciprocity that is always present when you give.

It doesn't matter if you are in debt or not, doesn't matter your age or any other factor.... Start saving NOW. Your best choices have gotten you where you are today. Change your life choices to create a lifestyle to live on less than what you make by saving before you spend. Many writers call this the automatic millionaire plan. Live on 70%-80% of what you bring home. Change your thinking about financial success and focus on cash flow. Focus on spending less than you earn. I get asked all the time if people should pay cash for a car or pay off their house. Normally the answer is no. These are assets but not investments. They should be viewed as part of your cash flow or an expense for using such items. You are much better off putting these funds in investments that will compound to grow to one day buy back your time.

Have you ever seen any of the cartoon movies that have those little yellow dudes called minions in them? Some have one eye, some with two and they work, work, work. Investments are like minions they work and replicate and compound. Why would you choose to put your limited funds into paying off a car or house which has simple interest when you could put your money in compound investments? The size of house you can afford or car you can justify is directly tied to where you are spending your money. Work all your outflows into living on less than 80% of what you earn. Do what you want with that

80% but save a minimum of 10% FIRST because if you try to save after you spend there will be nothing left to save. The 80% is used for all your living expenses including car and house payment. The lower the amount you live on the more you can save and the sooner you can buy back you time!

Warren Buffett says, "What you are doing when you invest is deferring consumption now to get more at a later time." If you constantly eat what you kill, one day you will starve because you will no longer be able to hunt. A simple thing to remember is short-term pain equals long term-gain and short-term gain means long-term pain. A couple of years ago, President Donald Trump passed a pretty substantial tax reduction that affected positively a very large portion of taxpayers. The IRS however issued new withholding tables to reflect the lower withholdings required as a result of the lower tax rates and for some people reduced their withholdings too much. Some taxpayers that were used to getting refunds at the end of the year broke even or owed a little. People all over the country were upset and thought their taxes went up solely based upon the change in their refund.

The facts were most of these people's bring home pay went up hundreds of dollars a month but they did not feel the affects of this increase because they were so used to spending everything they brought in. When they were showed that their total tax went down but amounts they prepaid through withholdings went down more, they didn't care. All they cared about was the "government" paid them less at the end of the year. Imagine you go into a fancy restaurant and the hostess takes your jacket to hang up. After dinner the hostess brings your jacket back and you jump up and down cheering that they gave you a jacket. IT WAS ALREADY YOUR JACKET. That is a silly story, I know, but people see their tax refunds the same way.

There is a strange psychological principle that comes into play with most people when it comes to what they spend. We all tend to spend what we have. We don't open our wallets and say, crap I have another $100 I need to get rid of, but we automatically adjust our lifestyle to whatever we have. The good news is this can work for us.

In 1990 when Lori was pregnant with our second son, we were approached by two of my bosses at the international CPA firm I worked at to leave that firm and move back to our hometown to operate an office for them. At that time, we both had jobs and Lori was on board with moving if she could quit her job and stay home with our kids. I ran the numbers and there was no way it was possible, but we took a leap of faith and went for it. We somehow adjusted our lifestyle to the available funds we had. When you start saving most of the time you do not really feel the impact. You automatically adjust your lifestyle to the amount you have. So start saving 10% now and test me on this.

```
        "Do not save what is left over after
      spending, but spend what is left after
                     saving"
               - Warren Buffett
```

If you save 10% of what you earn, at the end of 10 years you would have one years pay but that is only part of the truth. Every penny you save is a minion that works for you producing more minions. As soon as you get enough minions you can buy back your time because retirement doesn't take age it takes money. I have a good friend that retired at 38 because he kept his lifestyle at less than 50% of what he earned!!! He invested or delayed consumption more than half of what he earned into his business and outside income producing investments that allowed him to beat the "system" by 30 years!!!!

In his book Snowball, Warren Buffett "Discovered the miracle of capital – money that works for its owner as if it had a job of its own." As a young man he saved money and bought a pinball machine that he put in a barber shop and paid the owner a split of the funds he received. Isn't that a great idea especially from a kid? Buffett went further though, instead of spending his earnings, he used his profits to buy another machine! The fruits of the first pinball machine were replanted to produce more and more fruit. He discovered there is a difference between producing income and creating wealth. Wealth starts from the first penny you save like a seed. One seed over your life replicates thousands of times. Buffett knew that every seed he "consumed" was thousands of fruit that could be consumed in the future. Every dollar you spend on lifestyle today is a thousand dollars out of your wealth. You are not only consuming that dollar but all the dollars that would be made through compounding!!!

Warren Buffett also says, "The stock market is a great place to transfer wealth from impatient people to patient people." When I first read this, I was confused and thought Buffett was saying not to invest in the stock market. After further digging, I discovered the emphasis was on patience. Proper long-term investing is actually a predictable process, but a lot of people think to be successful you have to pick the right "stock" at the right time. This "speculative" style of investing is focused on short-term get rich quick and luck based decisions. This style of investing is very UNPREDICTABLE and extremely risky. Buffett teaches, don't make investment decisions based upon fear or greed. Investing should be based upon a predictable process and often the returns seem slow to come but like

EVERYTHING else in life success starts magnifying at a faster and faster pace the longer you are consistent. The problem is most people become IMPATIENT and jump ship before the real winnings pay off.

When people are in the accumulation phase of life, risk and volatility are their friend and should be harnessed through a concept called dollar-cost-averaging. The accumulation phase of life is when you are building your funds and are consistently contributing. You make the results of investing predictable by consistently investing monthly over a long period of time. For example, say you invest $100 in a stock that after 30 days is worth $50. Your value has gone down 50%. The bigger issue is that for you to break even, your stock now has to double ($50 to $100). However, if you invest another $100 you can now buy two shares giving you an average cost basis of $67 in the three shares you now own. By buying in again your stock only has to go from $50 to $67 to break even instead of doubling to $100. With consistent investing you can almost guarantee success. If your investments are up, YAY! If your investments are down, DOUBLE YAY, because you are buying them on sale and reducing your average cost basis thereby making it easier to make a profit. Of course, it is imperative to seek advice on how to pick a diversified portfolio, but then set it and almost forget it.

Even after you start down your path on the "automatic millionaire plan", you will be tempted to spend your gains and to make speculative investments or get rich quick. Stay the course and protect your minions. Remember, both when considering spending, and making risky investment decisions that a dollar spent or lost today equals a thousand dollars in the future. Have an "advance and protect" attitude. A good way to think when considering investment opportunities is it has to be either a "hell yes" or it is a no! Ask yourself, is the risk of loosing half of your minions worth the opportunity to double them? Generally, the answer to this should be an absolutely no. You worked hard to get where you are. You deferred consumption and adhered to the philosophy of short-term pain long-term gain. Do not let someone talk you into a risk that would erase all that you have worked for. If it sounds too good to be true, it is!

Early in my career, I was approached by a gentleman that presented me with an opportunity for investing into his business that factored receivables for medium sized companies that had contracts with large companies. The way it would work is company ABC would get a contract with Phillips Petroleum or some other company for say $1,000,000 which will take 90 days to get paid on. ABC would need money to get the job done and would "factor" or sell the right to be paid from Phillips to the gentleman's company in exchange for an advance of $900,000. When Phillips paid the $1,000,000 his company kept it all. It was basically a 90 day loan of $900,000 that he would make $100,000 in interest. He would make over 11% in 90 days which annualized is over 45% return. He of course needed money to fund these contracts and was willing to pay 2% a month to people that would invest with him. Wow 24% annual return on my money and Phillips Petroleum would pay him directly! What a deal! Right? Well as it turns out the contracts were made up and it was a Ponzi scheme where he would take new people's money to pay the interest due on other investors money never with the intention of paying any principle back. By paying interest he made everyone think things were going great and kept new referrals of money coming in. Eventually the FBI and IRS got involved and shut him down. People lost millions but the kick in the teeth was the government sued most of the people involved to get back some of the money "to reallocate" fairly to everyone. Of course they had to keep the vast majority of the funds to pay for expenses to make this "right" for everyone. Investors first got screwed by him then again by the government. It was an expensive lesson to learn but you can bet I will never forget, if it sounds too good to be true, it is.

Warren Buffett also says, "Be greedy when other people are fearful and fearful when other people are greedy." Man could I have used that advice when contemplating the factoring business investment! There IS such a thing called luck when it comes to being successful. Luck is not procrastinating when opportunity presents itself. Normally a good opportunity to hit a home run is one that most people walk away from because they are afraid to even step up to the plate. Most investors buy when the market is going up and sell when it is going down, completely opposite of what you should do. Opportunities present themselves when other people make irrational decisions based upon fear. One of my favorite quotes is from Tilman Fertitta in Shut Up and Listen, "When times are tough, eat the weak and grow your business." I know that sounds rude and intense but the reality is, home runs in the game of success are usually hit when times are tough and people are giving up or willing to sell things at a discount out of fear or from bad choices they made. When things are tough, tough people push through while others are quitting. When you see an opportunity, don't let fear keep you from advancing when other people are retreating.

Lori and I did not let fear of the unknown keep us from the incredible opportunity to buy our 25,000 sq ft house. Buying this home gave me instant collateral to leverage to continue the expansion of my CPA firm. It was exciting just to drive up the dirt driveway thinking that an Indian boy that grew up with a poverty, alcoholic and abusive family could even get someone to show me this house. The house had been for sale for multiple years and shown hundreds of times. I know that most people that had the ability to purchase this mansion decided not to even try because of all the unknown and fear of attempting to finish it out. Hundreds of realtors and builders had toured and passed on this opportunity. Was there risk, yes, but I made the decision to invest based upon value AND risk. There was no questioning that this home was an amazing buy and once finished would be worth double. There really was no speculation and the primary risk was not having the money to finish the home.

Should I have felt bad that the seller lost about 5 million dollars? Should I have felt bad that builders didn't attempt to purchase the house, finish it, and put several million in their pockets? Should I have felt bad at all the other people that missed out of the opportunity to get a literal mansion for pennies on the dollar? The answer is, what does how I feel or not feel have to do with making money? I did nothing wrong or immoral. I was not involved with the life choices that the seller made to put himself into a position that he could no longer afford to finish the home of his dreams. The fact is, how I felt, or my emotions had nothing to do with making a business decision? Repeat Warren Buffet's words "Invest based upon value and risk not greed or fear" over and over again.

Too many people follow their feelings, especially fear and greed, instead of pushing through and looking at the numbers and then acting in a way that if you get the deal, it is a hell yes and if not, you celebrate because it is a no. I did not pray for God to give me this opportunity but did pray for him to keep it from me if it was not end in a positive result. I pushed and modified and found creative ways to continue moving forward. Banks telling me no did not stop me. If I had not gotten the home, I could celebrate that he saved me from a bad deal.

My super-power, if you will, is finding a way to make opportunities that come my way into a hell yes! I seriously celebrate and thank God when I cannot make a deal work because in my mind he is saving me from myself. By having the attitude that it is either a hell yes or a no you help guard yourself from what Jack Welch in his book Winning calls "Deal Heat". Sometimes we get so excited about an opportunity we go plum stupid to make it happen. I have acquired 20 plus accounting practices so far. I know that for them to cash flow, I must verify collections, maintain control of client data once purchased and make sure the seller does not continue to do work behind my back. All very basic non-emotional concepts that have led to me being ultra-successful growing my business through acquisition.

In 2019 I started calling CPA practices in Catoosa, Ok where I had recently moved (into the 25,000 sq ft home). It makes sense that I lived there, so I should have an office there. I called the firm that I believed to be the largest in the area and asked if she had ever considered selling. This is a very standard call that I have made hundreds of times before and to no surprise to me she said no she did not want to sell. I generally take a no and follow up with a letter and one of my metal business cards planting a seed for the future if they ever get to a place they want to talk (they never throw away a metal business card by the way). In this case I followed up in a couple months and told her I would pay double what I normally would pay. Does that sound like it is based upon emotion OR the hell yes principle? STRIKE ONE! She again said no. I then decided that if she would not sell to me, I would buy the building she officed in and open an office next door to her. I don't ever just open an office and grow organically because it takes too long to be profitable. STRIKE TWO!

Faced with competing with me, she decided to sell to me at two times her collections from the prior year which she represented to me as $600,000 for a $1.2 million purchased price of which I gave her $300,000 up front. I was so excited I took her word and a draft of her tax return for what her collections were and drafted a contract accordingly. I did none of my normal due diligence! STRIKE 3! At the end of our first year of operations we only collected $80,000 from her clients and endured call after call of people that said they will only deal with her (apparently, she did returns while people waited which is an automatic no for me to acquire if I am told that). I am now faced with the decision of whether to sue her because there is no way possible that she had $600,000 of business that fell to $80,000 when my normal retention rate is about 90% of clients from an acquisition. Did you get that? But wait it, gets better. She came to me a few months after we took over and said she would knock off $200,000 from what I owe her if I could give her another $100,000 then. I knew that sounded too good to be true but did it anyway. STRIKE FOUR! I more that struck out of this deal all because I allowed my desire to have an office in Catoosa win! Making any decision based upon emotion almost always ends up bad and I knew better. I however do not obsess on my mistake because I always win. I either am successful or I learn. This was a very expensive lesson to learn that I will not be repeating.

Proverbs 21:20 (paraphrased) says "The wise man saves for the future but the foolish man spends whatever he gets." Those words come straight from God! Read that again. It matters less what you invest your savings in and more that you do it consistently and before you spend. Typical investments might include stocks, bonds, annuities, real estate, and insurance. I am not going to get in the weeds and do an in-depth discussion on what is proper and when, but I will give you three very important things to consider about any financial advisor giving you advice. You should seek the help of someone that is independent, who is a fiduciary, and is willing to show you their personal financial statement to prove they have achieved a level of success doing what they are proposing.

Independence is a principle that the advisor puts your interest above anyone or any company. In the traditional world of investing there are normally advisors that focus either on insurance or equity strategies. If you meet with an insurance person, they typically say you should never invest in equities because they are too risky. If you meet with an equity-based advisor, they say you should never invest in insurance because it is too expensive. The truth is they are both correct and both wrong. For the right person insurance or annuity products cannot be beat. For the wrong person they can be catastrophic. The same can be said for equity-based investments. If there is a sign above the advisor's door that says an insurance company's or brokerage firm's name you may need to question their independence. Who do they work for? Who do they answer to? Who dictates what advice they give you? A truly independent advisor can put your money with multiple insurance companies and or multiple equity companies and often makes recommendations that include both equity and insurance-based alternatives.

The advisor you choose should also be a fiduciary for their clients. A fiduciary is held to a standard that they are morally and legally bound to do what is right for you as their client. You can literally sue them if they do not act in your best interest. A fiduciary as compared to other financial advisors is like comparing a Certified Public Accountant to an unlicensed tax or accounting person. I am not saying they are better people, but they are held to a much higher standard in our legal system and have governing bodies that can sanction them or restrict them from continuing in business. Having an advisor that puts their very business on the line every day based upon doing what is right by their clients leads to less "selling" and more needs based advising.

When you spend money on advertising as a business owner, you are also investing. It is exactly the same as a farmer spending money on seed in the hopes of getting a good crop. When you invest in advertising you are planting "top-of-mind" seeds. People may not need your product or service right now but when they do, you want your business to "come to the top of their mind." The biggest issue I see with advertising is choosing what to spend your advertising dollars on. Success demands you be very intentional especially when it comes to investing or spending money on the "seeds" that grow your business. My business coach, Clay Clark, taught me to focus on three legs of a marketing strategy. The three legs represent where you will direct most if not all your resources.

The legs are chosen to maximize the potential exposure to your "ideal and likely buyer". In today's world maximizing Google search parameters has to be a focus for most businesses. People "google" search for everything. You want your business to be one of the top to pop up during searches. There are strategies that can help you get to the top that many people have written books on. Focus on your website be compliant with the latest requirements of search engines, getting reviews from as many people as you can, and writing content on your website. My best advice in this area is to contact Clay Clark's team at Thrivetimeshow.com.

Ultra success in life generally comes from leveraging time, people and money (I know I keep repeating this, haha). Save before you spend or you have nothing to invest, invest time in yourself to learn from other people's mistakes and victories rather than recreating the wheel, and advertise and promote yourself or your business in such a way that when people need you or what you sell, they think of you!

Albert Einstein once said, "Compound interest is the eighth wonder of the world. He who understands it, earns it.... He who doesn't ...pays it." Regardless of the investment vehicles you choose harness the power of compounding.

STEP #5: A DOLLAR SAVED TODAY CREATES $1,000 IN THE FUTURE. SAVE AND INVEST AND LIVE ON LESS.

Chapter 6:

CHECK THE FRUIT ON THE TREE

"You cannot become a master on your own"
-Jeff Goins The Art of Work

I was taught a long time ago to check the fruit on the tree from anyone giving me advice. I loved my mom and definitely owe a large part of my success to her life choices. She broke the generational bondage of alcoholism and abuse that had a life changing ripple effect for me, my sons, and generations to come. My dear mom, however had been married 6 times. I would seek my mom's advice on work ethic and many other things. If I needed marital advice, she is not the person I would go to!

This applies when you are picking a financial advisor or business coach ten-fold. If someone is going to give me real estate advice and they do not own any real estate, they may have book knowledge but no practical knowledge. Anyone giving you financial advice that is not where you want to be financially has not earned the right nor credibility to gain your trust. Ask anyone wanting to give you investment advice to see their personal financial statement. What have they done to accumulate wealth? Are they just an asset gatherer for an insurance or investment company? Are they investing in the same things they are recommending to you? Do they have their own financial plan?

My good friend and advisor Jim Stovall in his book, Millionaire Map, said "The best way to never reach your millionaire destination is to try to convince everyone you are already a millionaire. Don't be all hat and no cattle." Jim also warned me to be very wary of someone that calls themselves a consultant. Most of the time a consultant is someone that was not successful in whatever area they are offering advice in. Unfortunately, my experience is also that most "financial advisors" are all hat and no cattle!

Jeff Goins said "You cannot become a master on your own.... You learn from some people on purpose and some by accident. Your job is to recognize these teachers when they appear." Some people teach you what not to do and others teach you a better path. A lot of my success was learning what I didn't want in life based upon the lives lived by most of the people on both sides of my family. Remember the Crab story! You catch only one, you have to put a lid on the basket you place it in. If you catch more than one you can throw away the lid because every time one tries to climb out one of the others will reach up and pull it back down. Unfortunately, most of the time our friends and family act just like these crabs.

Surround yourself with success minded people that have a marriage like you want, a business like you want, a checkbook balance like you want, a house or other material things that you want, a heart for giving and sharing like you want, etc. Be intentional with who you listen to about everything important. People will come into your life at times you need them. I don't know if it is God, Buddha, the Universe or what, but my life experiences prove this true. Be alert and humble enough to recognize them and do as they say.

When I was 12 my mom married a man named Lewis Barcus. He was 6'4" and a total unathletic dork. At that time, I was getting into fights, shop lifting (mainly hostess deserts... don't judge me, I have a sweet tooth), and generally making some bad decisions. Lewis was not a man that at that time in my life I respected much. One time a group of kids showed up in our yard with the biggest and oldest one of them wanting to fight me. I was half his size and several years younger, but I never backed down from a fight. Lewis came out into the yard and in his typical nerdy way recommended we settle our differences through a game of volleyball!!! What???? Haha no volleyball was played that day but neither did we fight. In his strange way that day Lewis was the first man to ever stand up for me or step in and try to help me. He had my back albeit in a very docile way.

Lewis coached me in baseball and got me into Boy Scouts. He didn't really know anything about baseball or how to coach, but he was there. He was present in my life and was the first example of what a father and husband should be. He cheered my successes and tried to guide me through defeats. I knew I could count on him. Unfortunately, he was only in my life for a few short years. Lewis died of Cancer when I was 14 years old. His short time in my life opened my eyes to how I wanted to be as a father one day. His rapid departure also reinforced my thoughts and feelings that I could not count on anyone to be around for me. I knew I was on my own and was responsible for my own happiness and ultimate success. It was almost a cruel tease for God to allow me to experience the love of a father then take it away from me. The lesson I learned was, I could pick up little things from different experiences and people to make myself stronger but ultimately it was up to me and the "school of hard knocks" to find my way.

I think back on the people that have impacted my life and know many of them have no idea probably. I think about Mr. Kelly from fifth and sixth grade that always smiled and seemed to be able to make me feel better about myself. He had this strange way of always showing up at the right time. I also think about Mrs. Dawn Marie Colaw who saved my marriage and probably has no idea. Lori and I had been Married about 28 years and at the age of 45, I decided I "deserved" better. I laugh at myself as I type this even though it was a very difficult time because I literally prayed as a 12 year old boy for God to give me Lori. I guess I thought God made a mistake. I sought out a counselor that was faith based and had a long and successful marriage. Mrs. Colaw had the right fruit on the tree to earn the credibility for me to listen to her advice

In a short 30 minute session this tiny soft spoken woman of God taught me a life time of lessons in humility and vanity. I walked out of her office figuratively with a bloody nose, black eye and a heavy heart but also with the knowledge that I was an extremely blessed man to be married to a Godly woman like Lori who should have booted me to the curb so many times. I went to her seeking affirmation, and she had the spiritual and mental fortitude to lovingly punch me square in the mouth. People that are willing to say what is right even when they know it is not what you want to hear are priceless. Seek out people that have empathy for what you are going through and are not just a "yes man" when it comes to telling you what you need to hear.

So many people are willing to give you their opinions on all aspects of your life. Guard yourself and your mind from listening to them unless they have attained results that you strive for. Jim Stovall wrote "Never accept a map from someone who has not gone where you want to go. We live in a world where a lot is said and very little is done." If your financial advisor is broke, your personal trainer is overweight, your accountant is behind on his tax returns, or you are getting business advice from a consultant who has never been successful in any business, what can they actually teach you?

I have the honor of meeting with Jim on a monthly basis. He is a man full of wisdom and experience. The fact he gives me even a minute of his time humbles me beyond words. I do not feel worthy to sit and talk to him, but I relish the opportunity and do not waste a minute. Jim like so many successful people are willing to take time to pass on their life lessons through books, speaking and private counseling. There are people all around that will make themselves available if you will just ask. If given the opportunity, be respectful, timely and prepared.

Have specific questions to discuss and for gosh sake, shut up and listen.

If you occupy their time with your mouth moving it is not only disrespectful to them but also a waste of a golden opportunity. It only takes one sentence or statement to change your life or at least point you in a direction that allows you to continue moving forward. I think about a meeting I had with Mr. Stovall a month or so ago. Even though I am an accountant, I am a marketing person at heart. It is my job to grow and create opportunities for the many accountants that work for me. I was debating about a marketing campaign and asked Jim his thoughts. Like my meeting with Mrs. Colaw, I thought I knew what Jim would say. He directed me to go big or don't go at all. He continued saying that many people will go small and only one gets the top spot. I mean, who remembers who got second or third. Either be first or don't enter. His advice was totally opposite from what I thought. I did as he recommended. Instead of being one among many, I was placed at the top of the heap and was the focus of the entire event. That one piece of advice, whether you see the significance or not, will make me millions and save me millions on wasted marketing. Why spend a dollar to not get noticed when you can spend a thousand dollars and everyone notice you? Yes, you saved money doing just the dollar but you might as well burn it in the back yard.

"It is the mark of an educated mind to entertain a thought and not accept it"...... Aristotle.

Read that again. It takes an EDUCATED mind to hear something and not accept it. Be intentional with the advise you take and more importantly the people that you allow to give you advice.

STEP #6: YOUR SUCCESS WILL BE ACCELERATED BY SEEKING THE WISDOM OF OTHERS THAT HAVE ACHIEVED THE SUCCESS YOU DESIRE. BE WARY THAT THEY INDEED HAVE ACHIEVED SUCCESS IN THE AREAS THEY ARE OFFERING ADVICE.

Chapter 7:

YOU ARE YOUR BIGGEST ASSET

"You cannot expand your wallet
until you expand your mind"
-Jim Stovall, The Millionaire Map

If you get only one thing from this book and my life experiences, I hope it is that YOU can be, do, or have anything you want out of life. For YOU to succeed YOU have to change. Your biggest assignment from this book is to develop your biggest asset, YOU.

Along my journey of success, I have discovered something that seems very strange to me. I have a lot of friends that I would consider ultra- successful and every single one of them overcame struggles in life. I don't mean like they stubbed their toe a time or two climbing the success ladder. I mean alcohol, poverty, abuse, speech impediments, and drugs. We all tend to view success as a destination and therefore when we see a successful person we see where they are now and often can't imagine ourselves being there.

My experience is that people that have struggles actually have an advantage in reaching business and financial success over others. Pastor TD Jakes gave a sermon in which he stated, "Strength is built through resistance." Those of us that have had to push through rough times or circumstances build strength and often a tenacity that allows us to endure the down times on the road to success that might cause others to give up. I am not saying that a person that grew up in a middle or upper class home with two parents and never wanted for much cannot be successful. I am saying that if you had or are having struggles, they can either be the basis for an excuse or the energy to never quit.

Be the person who breaks the cycle of poverty, abuse, slothfulness, and unsuccess! And remember, PR consultant to the stars, Michael Levine says "Success in life is how you play the cards you are dealt. If you were born on 3rd base you didn't hit a triple!" My experience is it is easier for someone to start at home and work their way around the bases than it is for someone who was born on third to make it home! If that is true why do so few people that grew up with struggles reach success? Easy.... They see others or their circumstances as why they are not successful. They blame, complain and make excuses.

The secret to making it around the bases of success is to assume you are the source of your problems and commit to doing something about it. Circumstances do not make the man, they only reveal him to himself. You are not only your best asset, you are also your worst enemy. How you think, how you act, how you react to other people, how you react to your circumstances, what thoughts you allow other people to plant in your mind, how you see your chances for success, and most importantly how you talk to or about yourself.

One of the best books I have ever read was by Sean Stephenson titled Get Off Your But. Sean was born with a very rare and extremely debilitating disease that caused him to be only a few feet tall with extremely brittle bones. By all accounts he should have been an outcast full of self-pity and low self-esteem. Through the love and affirmation of his parents, Sean, however, grew to see his appearance and circumstances as uniqueness. He could be in a room and people would stare but he saw it as an opportunity to be unforgettable. Sean says, "If you believe you are ugly your mind will distort or ignore compliments and will find every shred of evidence proving you are ugly."

Sean nor I are saying live in some fantasy land when it comes to your strengths and weakness. On the contrary, be real with yourself but from a view of how to turn weakness into strengths. Instead of seeing weird, see memorable. Take a comprehensive inventory of your best asset (YOU) with a mind toward improvement instead of degradation. Think of taking a dirty beatdown car and turning it into a vehicle you can take out and show off. It is no more difficult to improve yourself than it is to rehabilitate a classic car.

Ken Schmidt, former CEO of Harley Davidson, once said in a speech I attended, "Success requires no apologies and failure permits no alibis. Success comes to those that become success conscious. Failure comes to those that allow themselves to be failure conscious." It is so true and so simple that most people cannot see it. Let me ask you this... If you met the President of the United States, how much respect would you show them with the words you used and how you referred to them? I am currently on our local CBS station every Monday for a segment where I answer viewers financial and tax questions. My wife and I enjoy eating out and it is very common for us to have people recognize me and literally treat me like a celebrity. They go out of their way to say hello and tell me how great a job I do. They call me famous and get excited that I am in the same restaurant.

Now contrast how you would speak to the President or other famous people with how you speak to yourself. Contrast the respect you give people you think are famous with the respect you show yourself. Sean Stephenson says "Try talking to yourself the way you would someone you respect or look up to. There is a 100% coordination between the words we use and how we feel (i.e. weird v. memorable)." He continues by saying "Happiness and confidence are massively affected by how you carry yourself...posture, facial expressions. It is almost impossible to be fearful without changing your posture and expressions when you are in a strong, confident posture. If you can shift the body, you can shift the mind." Are you getting this? You can literally change your circumstances by how you talk to yourself and how you carry yourself! If you are serious about being successful, do as I said earlier in this book and document everything about yourself. Video how you walk, record how you talk and what you say, document your thoughts and daily activities then critique yourself with an eye toward improvement. You can be the student and the teacher. Ask yourself what would I do right now if I were amazing? How would I dress, talk, and think? Then practice being amazing, and you will become amazing.

I am not one of those people that say just think it and you will achieve it, but it does all begin with your thoughts. I am very practical and systematic. Evaluate where you are today, in detail document the person you need to be to be successful, create a plan to change how you think and act then periodically measure your success. Athletes that want to be better study the skills of great players, video their movements and actions and compare themselves to greatness. They develop a practice schedule to create hand eye coordination and train muscle memory to be great. They are not born great they become great. Stop blaming and realize there is always something you can do to change your circumstances and it all begins with changing you. Be willing to accept the areas you need improvement AND the fact that you can improve those areas so you can take total responsibility for your future.

Tiger Woods is without a doubt one of the greatest golfers of my time and maybe all time. As I write this there are videos going around on social media showing how Tiger walks, swings the club, stands in between shots, and reacts to good and bad shots. These videos are shown side by side of videos of the exact actions by Tiger's son. His son moves and reacts almost exactly the same way. It is almost funny to watch them together. Even the way they scratch their nose is the same!!! If you want to be the best study every detail of the best and do what they do. I am not saying be a robot and loose who you are. You are unique. There has never been nor will there ever be someone exactly like you. You are perfect and precious in your own way, but we all have imperfections and shortcomings. To be better, take the gifts you have and emulate the strengths of successful people to build the best YOU possible.

Napoleon Hill said "Both poverty and riches are the offspring of thought." Mark Manson elaborated further in his book *The Subtle Art of Not Giving A F*ck*, saying "The rare people that become exceptional at something do so not because they think they are exceptional but because they are obsessed with self-improvement because they don't think they are that great at all. It is an ANTI-ENTITLEMENT attitude. They understand they are not already great. They are average but believe they can be so much better." Man oh man, you better read that again! Those two quotes summarizes the difference between successful people and those that quit on themselves. They don't have some super God given talent. They have just examined their limits and accepted that they can change if they choose to. Mark goes on to say "Growth comes from being wrong and making adjustments. Focus on thinking about what you could be doing wrong and how it could be done better. At one time scientists believed California was an island. Doctors believed that cutting yourself anywhere to make you bleed cured any disease. Women believed rubbing dog urine on their face had anti-aging benefits. Scientist believed fire was made out of something called Flogiston."

I attribute a very large portion of my success to a multi-level marketing business called Amway. Have you ever heard of them? They have been around for a very long time and developed a distribution system unlike any other. It gave people the opportunity to make money off of selling products and recruiting other people to sell and use products thereby creating a flow of products that didn't come from the store. They are structured like a lot of scam Ponzi schemes we have all seen. The difference is they are a true distribution system for moving products and you only make money off the movement of products and not off of recruiting people. When I saw their presentation I thought crap who wouldn't want to make money off of products they were buying everyday at grocery stores, Walmart, Target, etc.? I learned two life changing lessons from my time in the Amway business. First, I learned that my success was my responsibility and that it all started with developing ME. Second, I learned that most people are so lazy and unwilling to do simple things for success that a select few carried the load, and rightfully so, reaped the rewards. It is actually simple to be successful in America. Mark Levine told me that "All you have to do is show up sober and you will be more successful than most people. "

Amway was a venture where other people tied their success to mine. They did the work for me until I was ready. They showed me books to read, tapes to listen to and seminars to go to all designed to motivate and train me for success. They taught me life changing lessons like I could change me and that by changing me, I could be successful in anything I attempted. It also taught me that success is for everyone, but most people would rather fold laundry, watch television, sleep in on the weekends instead of invest in molding themselves to have a better future. I absolutely challenge you to find a distributor in the Amway business, join their organization, read the books, listen to the tapes, go to the seminars and work your butt off for a year building that business. You will learn how to deal with rejection, how to improve your attitude, and how to magnify your productive activity. You will get more in one year with them than in ten years in college. I bet you won't do it! I can honestly say it was challenging but absolutely the best learning and developing experience of my life.

If I might be blunt.... If you aren't as successful as you want to be but are not willing to do the things that are needed to become more successful, you ARE actually as successful as you WANT to be!

Mark Manson said, "The man who thinks he knows everything learns nothing. The more we admit we don't know the more opportunity we have to learn. Uncertainty is the root of all progress and growth." We all know plenty of "know-it-alls". It is a sad thing for me to meet these people but even worse to me is the person who knows they need to change and are not willing to put in the effort. I struggle to understand these people because most of the time they complain about their struggles but when presented with ways to change and grow they push back. I am saddened not because of where they are in life, but because I know in their mind, they have to be beating themselves up over their lack of effort. When you know you need to change but will not has to be the lowest point of self-esteem. Hopefully I am wrong.

Do you complain or do you train? My hope for you is that the time and effort I am putting into this book will cause you to see the incredible opportunities that stand in front of you. That you will believe my words to a point that you can no longer accept anything but excellence in your life. My prayer is that I can open the curtains of potential that lies inside you to a point that you can no longer tolerate anything but the best. The ripple affect for your family for generations to come stand in the balance. Take these steps not just for you but for your kids, grandkids and all the people they will touch.

Porsche made a marketing video back in 1995 that talks about that little voice that is inside all of us when we are kids. It is like a heartbeat deep down that tells us we can do anything. No matter where you were born, your race, your family we believe with no doubts that we can be an astronaut or President of the United States. At some point we stop listening to that voice. Life and the influence of others around us drown out that incredible voice of potential. Then one day when you are unloading the dishes from the dishwasher and you see your kids playing, you get a little glimpse of what you used to hear. The video then shows a Porsche sports car getting louder and closer and says, "Then you realize the voice is still there, It isn't too late, are you listening?" As I sit here in a Starbucks in Tulsa Oklahoma at 6:30 in the morning writing these words, I get chills and feel the emotion welling up inside me. You can do this!!!! Are you listening???? Can you remember the dreams and lack of doubt????

STEP #7: ALL SUCCESS BEGINS WITH YOU. BE PROACTIVE IN ASSESSING YOUR STRENGTHS AND WEAKNESSES THEN FOCUS ON IMPROVING YOUR BIGGEST ASSET, YOU!

Chapter 8:

GIVING IS AS IMPORTANT AS EARNING

"We are made by God like fruit with
seeds. We are made to share our gifts,
love, faith, and knowledge. Planting
seeds in others. There is no greater
occupation than to help others succeed"
-Pastor Joel Osteen

I have personally experienced two basic truths when it comes to being successful with money: (1) You will get when you give, and (2) you cannot be truly happy unless you share your blessings with others. Take those to the bank my friends. Most people equate success with how much they make which is normal. As you walk your path of success and make more money you will indeed upgrade where you live, where you eat, what you drive, what clothes you wear, etc. I promise you that all of that is great and motivating, but you will not find satisfaction. They are just things. A $300,000 car starts and drives to get you from point A to point B just the same as a $10,000 car.

Think about the anticipation and excitement of seeing your kids on Christmas morning opening the presents you gave them. Have you ever given them a present and they play with the box more than the gift? A bonus piece of financial advice... fill the box with foam peanuts and put something cheap inside, haha. Real joy comes from giving.

Jim Stovall told me a story a couple months ago about buying a million dollars worth of debt from debt collectors. Most people or companies do this to buy the debt cheap, collect on it and make a profit. Jim bought a bunch of medical debt. He then had letters written to all the people that owed the money telling them their debts were forgiven. Instead of trying to collect and make a profit, he blessed hundreds of people that had incurred medical debts.

Jim decided to call a few of the people to share in the blessings he had made possible. On one such call a man answered and when Jim introduced himself, the man yelled to his wife, "honey the man who paid for our daughter's eyes is on the phone." Jim asked what the man meant that he had paid for their daughter's eyes. The words Jim heard next gave me chills because Jim is a blind man and was told that this young girl needed surgery to save her eyesight and they could not afford it. A blind man's generosity saved a young girl's eyesight. Let that simmer for a minute. Jim has a handicap that he did not allow to hold him back. He used his handicap to solve problems for other people and created wealth. He then used his wealth to bless a young girl he never met to keep her from having the handicap he has. I use the word handicap because that is what our society would refer to Jim's blindness as. Even though Jim cannot see, he has vision. His vision allowed a little girl to see.

Movies and fable tales are full of people that are rich in money but are extremely unhappy. A lot of people think that if they just had more, they would be happy. That somehow money would solve all their problems. Happiness is about contentment and balance. I have met people that make well less than six figures that are very happy and people that make more than seven figures that are the most crabby people ever.

I personally like to set goals and then tie a reward to it. I LOVE sports cars. Did you know there is a whole class of cars called Super Cars? I think the super actually stands for super expensive! When Lori and I were involved with the Amway business they did things called dream building. We would go around and look at expensive houses and cars to stretch ourselves to try to find a trigger that would motivate us to work harder. Dream building is how I first saw the Porsche advertising video that lit my fire. It talked about the feeling of being in the car accelerating around curves. It had the sounds of the car as it sped up. It was the most amazing video I had ever watched. I wore that tape out. When I got tired and down for lack of results, I would watch that video and recharge to fight another day.

The day came that I hit my goal and went to the Porsche dealership to lease a brand new Turbo 911! It was bright blue and the sexiest car I had ever seen. I was on such a high! A few months after I got the car, I was driving my son to school and someone ran a stop sign and T-boned my beautiful dream car. Immediately after, I did not think of my car, I thought is my son alright. At that moment God taught me that while material things are great, they come and go, but my son cannot be replaced. I actually smiled as I got out of the car knowing that what was precious most to me was okay.

After the Porsche, I set a goal for a bright orange McLaren MP4-12c. The doors open up instead of out. I was very surprised that there was a car that would excite me more than the 911 Turbo. Of course (being a good Oklahoma State University fan), I wanted an orange one. Volcano Orange to be exact. I first saw this car in a magazine with both doors open sitting in front of a private jet. It cost $200,000 used. I set a goal but didn't really believe I would ever be able to buy one.

I did indeed hit my goal and started looking for what was now the car of my dreams. These cars are not sold at dealerships anywhere near Tulsa, Oklahoma so all shopping was done online. I looked and looked but could not find a Volcano Orange McLaren. I had to have the Volcano Orange one because it was the one I had focused on for so long. My victory would not be as sweet with any other color. I was about to give up and buy a different Sports car when I found a McLaren in Chicago that sounded perfect but they did not list the color. I emailed the dealership and anxiously awaited their reply. The next day they finally responded and it was Volcano Orange! My wife and I drove to Chicago the next week and drove it home.

Not a year later McLaren came out with a car called a 720S. Holly cow it was gorgeous. You guessed it, I had found a new "car of my dreams." The more successful you become the more you realize that there is always a newer and better dream car, dream house, more expensive clothes, etc. Material things are not a destination nor are they a determining factor of happiness. There will always be something better and thus you will never achieve contentment through getting things. I know, I know we have all heard this kind of talk before. I do think there is a point in the path of success that material things properly play a role in creating motivation. The trap is getting wrapped up on always wanting more or better. What I want you to learn here is at some point in time your drive and motivation has to be based on giving and not getting. If you never transition away from getting more, you will not be able to achieve true contentment and happiness. We are all created to serve, and it is in our very DNA to feel good when we give and do for others.

Be proactive with a plan to give just like you do for developing yourself and growing your success. You will actually get more "warm fuzzy feelings" from planning to give than you do planning to achieve. People that give out of spite or because they are required to miss the point. Give in ways that give you joy. Bless others and share in that blessing. Do not give to glorify yourself to others but don't hide those actions either. You will inspire others to give by sharing the joy. Isn't that the purpose for planting seeds? To turn one seed into a harvest. Your giving, if done properly can glorify God, create motivation in others to give, and create passion and joy inside you that the most expensive car on the planet cannot.

A few years ago, we decided to send $100 dollar bills to 200 randomly selected clients with a letter that said it is a time to be thankful and I wanted to share our blessings with them. The letter instructed the recipients to spend it on themselves or if they wanted to receive double benefit from the gift from us, to give the money away, pay for someone's groceries. To pay it forward if they wanted to experience the full joy of our gift. We also asked them to send me an email to tell me what they used the money for. We gave to bless others, planted a seed in them to give it to someone else to give themselves more joy than spending, and asked that they share their story to give us joy in how our seeds grew.

Jim Stovall wrote a book called The Gift of Giving. In it he writes that there is reciprocity in giving. This was a difficult thing for me to understand. My religious upbringing taught me that you should give without expecting anything in return. That it was wrong to glorify ourselves through telling everyone what we did. I thought Jim's words were contrary to what I had been taught all my life, but they aren't. There is a difference in saying "look what I did" and let me share in how I was blessed by blessing others to motivate others to do the same. Give not to celebrate how "selfless" you are, but to genuinely plant seeds in the lives of the recipient as well as others that will join you in giving.

Whether you think it is God, Jesus, Buddha, Karma or whatever, you will get when you give if done with the right frame of mind and heart.

"Test Me now in this," says the Lord of hosts, "If I will not open for you the window of heaven and pour out for you a blessing until it overflows"

-God in Malachi 3:10

The creator of everything literally says I dare you to give! When you are sad, stressed, or face challenges go give and serve others and see if your attitude doesn't change. When you give you are showing God or nature, or whatever you believe in, that money is just a vehicle to accomplish things, it does not define who you are, and you understand that by giving, you are sharing the fruits of your labor. It shows you do not love money and trust that you will be able to make more.

I watched a video at church once that showed a bunch of people sitting at a table with a pie. The pie got passed around as people took a piece out. The pie got around to the last two people and there was only one piece of pie left. The last person at the table represented God. The person before God had to make a choice to finish off the pie or give God a slice. He chose himself and as he took the last piece someone at the table said, "dude but he (God) brought the pie." I do believe that God gives us all abilities to create wealth (however we each define it). He created a world where to be truly happy and create more we have to share our gifts with others. We honor God by both creating and giving. The word work in Hebrew actually means worship.

Jim goes on to say that you should plan how you give. Give in a way that you enjoy. Give in a way that creates pathways for you to make more money to be able to give more. For instance, being a lover of sports cars, I had a 1964 Daytona replica race car built. I got to be involved and watch as it came together. I got to test drive it multiple times. When it was complete, we announced that we would be auctioning off the car at a large national auction and donating all the funds to St Jude's Children's Hospital. We had a car show at one of our offices with the Daytona right in front with signs that it was being auctioned and donated. Two of the local major television stations did feel good stories on the car. When it was auctioned off, we took pictures and videos to post all over social media.

I could have just written a check, but by giving the Daytona I got to enjoy being involved when it was created and received a ton of publicity for my business. I got to bless families dealing with the worst thing possible in having their young child be sick and magnify the joy through doing it in a way that motivated others to give, got my staff at my office involved and literally helped my business grow. It is a proven fact that people like to do business with businesses that give back.

During the Covid pandemic most restaurants were struggling as people were too afraid to go out. In Oklahoma the insides of most restaurants were closed but delivery and drive throughs were open. My firm redirected our marketing money on radio to help out by saying that if people went out to eat or had delivery, they could send us their receipt and we would mail them a check for up to $25 for their meal. We committed $50,000 to the first two thousand people that sent in receipts. By giving in this way we helped the restaurant owners and employees and helped keep commerce going. Restaurants all over our area actually had signs they put up with our offer, television, radio and print media did stories on it and we again posted it on social media. We gave back, helped our community, and created publicity for our business. Sure, I could have written a check to local food banks but giving this way sowed seeds in creating income for people that would spend in other businesses and grew our business.

The Bible says, "God sends seed to the sower." Think about that. What is a sower? It is a person that plants seeds in order for those seeds to grow and multiply. If you only benefit yourself and your family, are you planting seeds or consuming what you create? By giving you are planting seeds in the lives of others that will bloom far into the future. My entire purpose on this planet is to create ripple effects in people's lives. By helping one person and changing their life, I am also potentially changing their kids lives, their brothers lives, their grandkids lives and all the lives that all those generations of people touch. By being intentional in how I give, I can give people the opportunity for a hand up instead of just a hand out and motivate others to do the same.

I try to give not only in ways that I enjoy but also in ways that can create that ripple effect. I support multiple charities that don't just give handouts, they teach people to create a life that is better for themselves. Charities that take funds to Africa and teach people how to own businesses and be self-sufficient. Those people then in turn will teach others to do the same. The Bible also talks about teaching a man to fish instead of giving a man a fish. Being charitable can actually hurt people and thus you are planting negative seeds.

Giving handouts are great but if that is all we do then people become reliant upon us. In most national forest in this country there are signs to not feed the animals because they will become reliant upon us for their future. We do the same thing to the poor in this country. My mother was on welfare, and we used food stamps, but she took it as a hand up to help her get training to get a career. Most of my family are lifetime welfare people. We are absolutely called to help those that need our help but if we do it properly, we can sow seeds in their lives and the lives of generations to come.

STEP #8: GIVING IS THE KEY TO HAPPINESS AND CONTENTMENT. PLAN HOW YOU GIVE TO BLESS OTHERS, ENCOURAGE OTHERS TO GIVE, AND UNDERSTAND THERE IS RECIPROCITY IN GIVING.

Chapter 9:

PIGS DON'T KNOW PIGS STINK

"... Guard what God has entrusted
to you. Avoid godless, foolish
discussions with those who oppose you
with their so called knowledge"
-God in 1 Timothy 6:20

One of the things that changed my life the most was the inspirational tapes I listened to while involved with the Amway business. One such tape was a speech by Dave Severn titled Pigs Don't Know Pigs Stink. This two-hour presentation opened my eyes as to why many of my friends and family seemed to be trying to hold me back. They not only did not compliment or encourage me, they went further and made comments about how impossible it is to be successful, how I was dumb for working hard or taking risks. You would think that those that love you and know you would be your biggest cheerleaders, but they often are not.

The problem is just like pigs don't know pigs stink, the closest people to us often do not know their attitudes and life choices stink. Our family and friends only know the world they live in which is often filled with excuses and blaming. Most people cannot face up to the fact that their current circumstances are a direct result of the decisions they have made in their lives up to that point. We live in an entitlement and excuse making world. It is easier to blame others for their lack of success than to own their choices. As soon as you try to better yourself, someone usually reaches up and pulls you back down with words that seem to make sense but serve to deflate your ambitions. When you make excuses and are unwilling to make changes you are choosing your situation. When you go further and defend your circumstances as they are, you are making a case for staying right where you are. When you do not choose to get better, you are actually choosing to stay just as you are. Someone that says they want to get in shape but will not change how the eat and drink, is actually saying the food and drink they consume is more important to them than being healthy. They are CHOOSING to be overweight. It is their choice to make but most will then blame their age, genealogy, stress or some other thing for the results of their choice. They are not bad people by any means. God gave them that body for them to do as they please. The point of fact is we all make choices that create results. You cannot have different results without different choices. I am not saying any one person is better or worse than another. I am simply saying your life, your choices, your consequences.

On your journey to success, you must question everything you think you know because what you know was learned from others that generally have had the same life experiences you have had. Literally you don't know what you don't know and what you do know might be completely incorrect. If you want to win, accept being judged by others that are often closest to you and not let them get to you. In my early days, I thought it was okay to steal (unless you got caught haha), it was okay to smack people around that disagreed with you to get your way, and the strongest and biggest made the rules. As my mom got us away from some of the family and friends that were shaping my thoughts and habits, I learned that normal people did not steal and fight all the time. My baseline for what was normal and acceptable began changing as the people surrounding me changed.

I distinctly remember one day in the lunch room when I was in the 8th grade hearing a group of boys talk about brushing their teeth and having white teeth. I obviously knew what a toothbrush was but never really used it. Most of the adults in my family had false teeth, I never heard of any of them going to the dentist unless they were in pain. It was not a habit that was taught to me or had any type of priority put upon doing it. Obviously today, I understand that personal hygiene is very important, and it is a given part of everyday life. Normal people brush their teeth, take showers, and change their clothes. Back then my normal was the complete opposite and I had no other way of knowing it should be any other way. Haha, literally pigs didn't know pigs stunk.

Our brains are constantly changing and rearranging how we feel and think based upon our experiences and more importantly how those around us react to those experiences. Our thoughts create actions which create habits which define our potential for success.

I have heard it said that the best thing you can do for the poor is not be one. Acknowledge that to have a different life you make different choices. Forgive me if this sounds rough but, like me, you may have to do EVERYTHING completely different than how you have seen done by those that you have grown up with. Earlier in this book we discussed assessing everything you do, say, and think. I would go further and suggest that you study people that have what you want. What they do on a daily basis, how they talk, how they think and then compare that to your "norm." Document what your family has taught you the normal way to act is and see if that lines up with how successful people act. Please know this, I am in no way saying that I am now better than any of my family or old friends. I am saying that I made different choices than most of them and thus have a different life today than they do. More important to me, my kids and future generations have different lives than they would have had.

I believe Zig Ziglar once said "If you always do what you have always done, you will always have what you have always had." Those simple words could change your life if you actually understand their meaning. To have and be different, you must be and do different. It is not as simple to do as it sounds though because usually the habits and thoughts that created the life you have are often very deep and ingrained into your total being. I often think about racism of whites to blacks and yes blacks to whites. Racism is not limited to only one race. I have experienced being the only white kid in class and was treated just as differently as a single black child in an otherwise all white class. Thinking I am better than someone else just because of the color of my skin is such a foreign thought to me that I cannot imagine people actually thinking that way. There is no way possible for someone to justify the validity of thinking that way to me, but people still think that way.

One day while meeting with a CPA in a small town in Texas as a part of my due diligence to potentially buy his accounting practice, the CPA made a racist remark. I sat there silent for what seemed to be several minutes arguing with myself in my mind as to whether I had just really heard what I heard. It was so shocking and surprising to me and I was stunned. First, I thought people no longer thought that way and second thought, why did he think it was okay to make such a remark to me? Yes, my complexion is white, but my grandfather was full blood Indian and was so dark complected that often people thought he was black. This was the year 2021. How could anyone still think that way? That pig definitely did not know he stunk. It was a natural statement that flowed right out of his mouth.

After I had a chance to gather myself, my next thought was the person that I had selected to come to this office and run it was half black. I never really thought about him being black. I did not define him as a half black person, he was just a very sharp young man that had been practically a part of my family and a very close friend of one of my sons for years. As I composed myself, I still had hope that I heard him wrong. I told this CPA that we had an amazing young professional that I planned on having move to Texas and run his office and that he was half black. I asked if he thought that would be a problem. He responded that he thought it would be better if we had someone there that looked more like me and him!!! I thanked him for his time and excused myself. I called the broker that was listing this business and told him what happened and that I would not be buying.

Racism is not the subject of this book but right then and there this experience provided a reminder of how completely different other people's thoughts and beliefs can be. That man thought nothing was wrong with how he thought and the words he spoke. That was his "norm." In his mind he was right. I would image (or hope) that every person reading these words understands just how wrong his thoughts are. To a much lesser degree, we all have thoughts and beliefs that are just as wrong, and we do not know it. This chapter is an attempt to help you acknowledge that there are things that stink about you that you don't even know stink.

The person who thinks they know everything is able to learn nothing new. Your family and friends think they know what is best and right about your potential, but they are wrong if those thoughts place a limit upon you or themselves. Embrace the idea that pigs don't know pigs stink. The more you admit that you don't know, the more opportunity you have to learn. As Mark Manson says, "Uncertainty is the root of all progress and all growth."

STEP #9: DO A DEEP DIVE ON EVERYTHING YOU THINK AND KNOW. WHAT YOU KNOW YOU HAVE LEARNED FROM YOUR EXISTING ENVIRONMENT AND OFTEN TIMES PIGS DON'T KNOW PIGS STINK (INCLUDING WHAT THEY THINK IS TRUE AND FALSE ABOUT THE WORLD AROUND THEM).

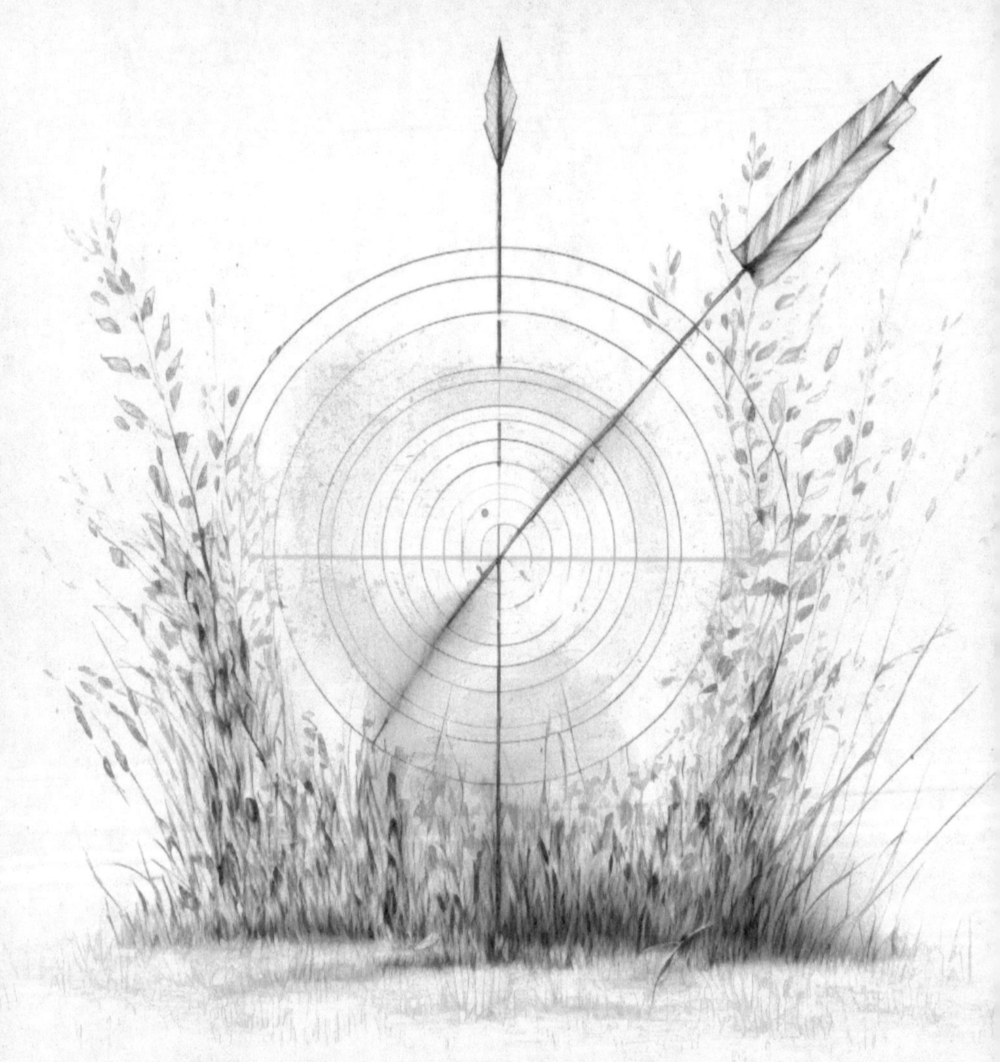

Chapter 10:

DEFINITENESS OF PURPOSE V. DRIFTING

"Success requires no apologies and
failure permits no alibis"
-Ken Schmidt
(former Communications
director-Harley Davidson)

Warren Buffett said, "We all won the ovarian lottery just being born in this country." I contend it is both a blessing and a curse because you can drift though life in the US and live better than 95% of the people in the rest of the world. As stated earlier, most of the ultra-successful people I have met fought through some sort of struggle. They were overcomers of poverty, abuse, alcohol or drug addiction. People that are forced to overcome or suffer often are more focused to get away from that life. They become fighters through their circumstances. These people have separated themselves from other people suffering similar circumstances that have chosen to have a victim mentality and blame others for their plight in life. Overcomers like my mother who said nope I will not be abused or stay married to an alcoholic. She would not accept that just because her entire family spent most of their lives "playing" the system to take handouts instead of a hand up, that was her only option.

The people I feel most sorry for are those that have had a decent life without much struggle. These "cushy life" people on average seem to be more apt to drift or coast through, settling for a simple less driven life. I can almost understand people that have had to struggle and choose to blame others because that is what they have been taught by their friends, family and frankly our government. But people that have all the opportunity in the world and don't take advantage of the gift they have at their fingertips are beyond my comprehension.

Napoleon Hill's masterpieces, Think and Grow Rich and Outwitting the Devil, explain why some people achieve success and others do not. If you do just one thing from reading this book and you are serious about changing your life read those two books by Mr. Hill. When you can get focused on what you want and how to get it, you are unstoppable. Strive to create your life actively instead of passively seeing what life brings to you. These two books are polar opposites of each other. While Think and Grow Rich discusses definiteness of purpose and unwavering desire, Outwitting the Devil illustrates the dangers of having no purpose and goes so far as to say drifting is Satan's primary tool for evil.

Multiple times in this book I have mentioned writing down where you are right now and where you want to go, as well as studying your weaknesses that would stand in the way of your progress. Your journey to success needs these two points on the map of your life documented. If you are not willing to do the simple things you don't deserve the rewards. The problem is most people in this country focus on short term gain which almost always leads to long term pain. Think about what you did today, yesterday, last week. How much did you read instead of watching television? Who did you spend your time with and do those people have the life you want? Are you just drifting through life doing the same thing as you did the week before and the week before that? The definition of insanity is doing the same thing over and over again and expecting different results.

In his book The Outliers, Malcolm Gladwell details the success of people in sports, music and business and shows that it takes 10,000 hours of doing something to become an expert. Are you willing to put 10,000 hours into achieving the life you want? It takes time to change who you are in order to even recognize what it takes to be successful. Most people in our instant gratification microwave oven society, want everything now and sees success as a destination instead of a journey. Sheer persistence is often the difference between success and failure. I have heard it put another way. Intensity is the price of excellence. Have an attitude that you are planting today so you can harvest tomorrow. Can you imagine a farmer planting seeds then quitting because he didn't get a harvest the following week or month? Invest the 10,000 hours in changing YOU. Become an expert on YOU. Who are YOU, where are YOU compared to successful people, what changes do you need to make to be all that YOU were meant to be or capable of being, and how do YOU define success? Create a survey of questions to ask other people about YOU just like a business does about their products. Be intensely focused on developing YOU!

The statistics that I have seen are that the average person watches six hours of television a day and is on social media in excess of five hours a day! Most people's lack of success is not because of their background, heritage, family history or what political party is in office. It is lack of vision, lack of purpose and lack of intensity. The sad truth is there is a proven path to success that pretty much anyone in this great country can walk. Some never hear there is a path, some hear there is a path and don't believe it really works, some will start down the path and quit prematurely because of roadblocks or setbacks and a small few will refuse to quit. Adversity is a seed for future success, but the average person gets knocked down once or twice and quits.

When my son and I were preparing for the body building competition, I had pain, soreness, and adversity. My coach had to remind me that I was actually breaking down my body and forcing it to do things it didn't want to do. My body and mind fought me along the way. To build muscle you break it down and it gets stronger as it repairs itself. To burn fat you force the body to use reserves of energy it has built up for the future. There was constant pressure to eat wrong, take the day off, or quit early. My success in that competition was not dependent on anything except my unwavering desire to succeed. To succeed meant doing the simple things consistently and not quit. I don't understand why one step back takes five steps forward to get back to square one. I have said when I get to meet God, I am going to ask him why one candy bar, that takes five minutes to eat, takes two hours to burn off. Success in anything has this same lopsided formula. Recognize that failure is easy and comfortable but creates a life of pain and regret. Success is just as easy but comes to only those that can "lock in" on consistently doing the small things week by week, day by day, hour by hour.

"Most people can be relatively successful because we are born at a time where all you have to do is show up sober because most of your competitors are stupid and lazy." Michael Levine's words in that statement cut to the heart of the blessing and curse of living in this great country. The difference between successful people and average people really isn't that great. Dedicate an hour of your day to change how you think for 21 days and you will see small improvements. Remember, action creates motivation, not the other way around. While training for the body building competition or the marathon, all I focused on was my feet hitting the ground within five seconds of my alarm going off. There were days I made positive progress but there were many days I actually went backwards. It was often two steps forward one step backwards.

The thing that set me apart from most people that attempt anything in life is that I did not question IF I was going to do what I said I was going to do. The only question was how long was it going to take for me to get to the destination. This attitude of unwavering desire and definiteness of purpose (or a refusal to give up attitude) allowed me to take setbacks and say why did I fail and what can I do next time to not fail. Do you think people that climb mountains just woke up and went out and climbed to the peak? No! Most, if not all, studied what it would take to be successful, identified the shape they are in physically and mentally, trained with people that had done it before, and started small to push themselves beyond their limits to grow. Up to the day of the marathon, in all my training I never actually ran 26.2 miles. I ran several 5ks, a 10k and a half marathon. I had victories and failures along the way, but NEVER ONCE did I think I could not or would not run the marathon. I am not special at all. Anyone can change their attitude and understand success is a definable place and the only person keeping them from that place is themselves. The first step is writing it down because if it isn't written down it isn't real. Make the destination fixed and unchangeable and you will be able to accept setbacks along the way. Creating the mindset that you will not quit is more important than the physical side of anything.

Jeff Goins in The Art of Work says, "A calling goes beyond what you think your abilities are and calls into question your potential. The risk of not committing is greater than the cost of making the wrong choice along the way. When you fail you learn. Failure is a friend dressed up like an enemy." That is wisdom right there. That is the "secret sauce" to success. Create a mindset of expecting to reach your goal then plan your path in a way that you literally demand you succeed. Total failure only happens when you lose sight and quit. Failing along the way is not negative. It is opportunities to get better, stronger, and more determined. Fight on in the face of discouragement. The battle is won, one fight at a time. As my business coach Clay Clark always says, in success there is no hocus pocus just maniacal focus.

Don't judge yourself on the outcome. Your success is dependent upon what you did today verses what you needed to do. Judge yourself on how deliberate and intentional you were day by day, minute by minute. If you say no to that candy bar, your sacrifice in that small choice saved you two hours of extra work out. That choice is the victory not what the scale says. Build victories on top of victories to create a consistent life of maniacal focus. YOU can change YOU one choice at a time.

STEP #10: CREATE A NO QUIT ATTITUDE BY BEING MANICALLY FOCUSED AND INTENTIONAL WITH EVERY DECISION YOU MAKE. FIGHT THE EASY CHOICES THAT LEAD TO DRIFTING AND FOR GOD'S SAKE, READ NAPOLEON HILL'S BOOK THINK AND GROW RICH MULTIPLE TIMES!

Chapter 11:

BE WILLING TO JUMP OUT OF THE AIRPLANE AND ASSEMBLE THE PARACHUTE ON THE WAY DOWN

"Well Begun is Half Done"
Aristotle

In the previous chapter we discussed identifying where you want to go and set it in stone. Do not waiver on where you are going and just start moving. Action is your focus not whether you will reach your goal. There are a lot of people in life that identify their "target," but never pull the trigger for fear of missing. They are "ready, aim, aim, aim, aim" people. It is much better to do something and fail thereby learning from the mistakes made instead of never doing anything.

My Pastor, Craig Groeschel, did a sermon where he discussed small victories are the secret to staying the course. He told a story that said that the secret to success is flossing your teeth. Sounds silly doesn't it! His contention is that when you floss your teeth you feel good because you know most people don't. When you feel good about yourself you are more apt to get up and exercise the next day. When you exercise you are more apt to eat right. When you eat right you are healthier and have more energy and are more attentive at work and at home. If your goal is to be more successful at work, then floss your teeth! Small victories lead to more small victories. All the small victories add up to equal big victories.

Success breeds success. When we are counseling people to get out of consumer debt, the first step is to make a list of all the credit card and other debt they have. They are instructed to put at the top of the list the ones with the lowest balance. Most people make just above the minimum payment on all their cards. We instruct them to pay minimum payments on all but the card with the lowest balance. They are taught to apply all the excess payments to the lowest balance to pay it off first. Then take the amount they were paying on the first card and add it to the next smallest card till it is paid off, continuing through all the cards from smallest to largest. When the first card is paid off, we tell them to celebrate that victory because paying off the smallest is the hardest step because it is the step that they change their frame of mind about debt for the rest of their lives. By working their plan and gaining the small victory early, they are encouraged to continue to the next one and the next one.

Small victories come from taking action. Action creates results. Good results are a win, but bad results are a double win because you learn and are stronger for the next action. Do not underestimate the small steps. Action creates habits and habits decide your future. We are all exactly where we are in life because of the habits we have developed through the actions we have taken day to day. You don't need to know the exact path you will take from where you are today to where you want to go. You just have to act. Be willing to step out of the airplane and assemble that parachute on the way down. When you are faced with adversity you can either cave under the pressure or rise to the occasion. Change is tough and I promise you do not have all the answers, nor do you need to know all the answers. You simply need to know where you want to go and then move.

Successful football coaches focus on getting the next first down even though the goal is scoring a touchdown. To get the next first down, the lineman must make their blocks. To make their blocks, lineman must take the first step correctly to open their hips the right way to gain the leverage needed to move their opponent. The first step to victory then, is to practice over and over the first step of a play. A person trying to lose weight sets their goal weight. Frustration sets in daily when they step on the scale and measure what they think success should look like. The person that successfully loses weight however focuses on the battle to eat right for breakfast, walking past that box of donuts the sweet secretary brings to the office or drinking a glass of water instead of that yummy Mountain Dew! I say that as I shove a big bite of homemade cinnamon role in my mouth. Don't judge me it is the day after Christmas and I don't want them to go to waste, hahaha!

Fear of change and the unknown is a killer of a lot of dreams. A great book on change is Who Moved My Cheese by Spencer Johnson. It is a story of two little people and two mice that live in a maze and survive on cheese. Their entire world is centered around having cheese and how they react when they run out of cheese. It is a must read and contains statements like:

"Expect Change and Look for It;"

"Expect Change and be ready to adapt to it;"

"Movement in a new direction helps you find new cheese;"

"When you move beyond fear you feel free;"

"Imagining myself enjoying new cheese before I
find it leads me to it;"

"The quicker you let go of old cheese the sooner
you find new cheese;" and

"What would I do if I wasn't afraid."

I hope that the common theme that you are seeing in this book is that you can be as successful as you want to be, but you must be willing to take that first step even though you may not know what the third, fourth or fifth steps look like. Be willing to change even though change is intimidating. Focus on small steps to gain small victories and keep moving.

By focusing on small victories, you are moving the measuring stick that determines success closer and thus the victory is easier to hit and celebrate. When your action creates small victories, you allow yourself to create motivation to continue. Focusing on the big goal will create frustration and justification to quit. Just like in target practice, you may not hit the bullseye, but you will have the small victory of at least hitting the target. As you gain confidence and experience you start hitting the center of the target and can slowly move the target further away. If you want to get frustrated start immediately with the target far away. Missing the target is not the worst thing, not taking the shot is. If you do not take the shot, you can not learn and adjust. You will not be an expert marksman by being a "ready, aim, aim, aim" person. Be a "ready, aim, fire, adjust" person.

Set long-term goals that seem unattainable then back them down to very short-term goals. Focus on the success of reaching the short-term goals and build goals and victories on top of each other. Clay Clark teaches his call center people to be willing to make one hundred calls to get one yes. Get excited when you get a no to learn from the experience and to get that much closer to a yes. Success is simply a string of failures by a person continually moving forward learning and adjusting as they go. Someone that is more successful than you has just failed more. You will only see the end result of someone else's actions, but the scars of failure and defeat are there. Remember when a person builds muscle, they are actually breaking down and scaring their existing muscle. I heard a speaker one time say that success is like being pregnant. People see the result but do not know how many times you got screwed (sorry but paints a vivid picture doesn't it). People that cannot start can never finish.

There really are three paths to success, be born with an extreme God given talent (like in sports), win the lottery, or be intentional and deliberate about working the time proven pattern for success. No one achieves success accidentally unless they are born with it or are extremely lucky. Success is intentional and deliberate and requires tenacity because even though there is a pattern that is predictable, how long it takes varies from person to person. I assume that the fact you are reading this book, you are like me and do not qualify for success under the first two paths! Thomas Edison is quoted as saying "Opportunity (success) is missed by most people because it is dressed in overalls and looks like work."

There is such a thing as luck in success though. Remember luck is being presented with an opportunity and not procrastinating. Being prepared and motivated are overrated. Jump out of the plane and move forward. Opportunities will "magically" present themselves when you leap out in faith towards a better life. I think the old saying that when the student is ready the teacher will appear is all about stepping out and taking a chance even if you don't feel you know all of what it takes to succeed. Remember John Paul Jones' statement, "Those that will not risk cannot win."

All great discoveries started with someone pursuing an unknown. They learned along the way. The exciting thing I have experienced is that as you move forward, the destination may change. You may discover things along the way that move your ultimate target. You literally do not know what you do not know but you will never find out what you do not know unless you start moving forward!

As I continue on my personal path to reach my goal of having a $50 million dollar accounting firm, the fear of the unknown still chases me. The fourth quarter is the best time of the year to acquire accounting firms for the seller but the worst financially for the buyer (ME). Most of the revenue in my line of work is earned between January 15 and October 15. During the slow periods of November and December staff members still want paychecks and rent still has to be paid. In the last 45 days, I have ran through six hundred thousand in operating capital. My biggest risk is running out of money during the slow periods.

A month or so ago I read Andy Stanley's book Visioneering. I always look for just a few "nuggets of knowledge" that can move me forward. Andy wrote this book to help people find their vision and to see if their vision is in line with God's vision. The huge nugget I gained from his book is that if my vision is in line with God's, my vision is therefore just a small piece of his. If it is ultimately God's vision, then he, at a minimum, shares in the responsibility for it's ultimate success. It isn't all up to me to find the people that will help, it isn't all my responsibility to find the next practice to purchase or bank to give me funding, or to develop the systems to ensure success. I do have to keep moving forward making mistakes and learning from them all with the confidence that God will help me find and learn a way. I still feel the pressure to perform, but when times are uncertain, I can tell God okay this is your plan too, I need some help and believe he will deliver. What better partner in business can I have other than God.

I believe he is a God of excess success for those willing to leap forward in faith and understand that money is a tool to achieve his goals with and for him. I do not always know what is on the other side of doors of opportunity presented to me, but believe I will either learn from it or it will get me one step closer to achieving my goals. Have the attitude that you can only fail by quitting. You will NEVER have all the answers so jump and start assembling.

STEP #11: BE A READY, AIM, FIRE AND ADJUST PERSON. DON'T WAIT TILL YOU HAVE THE PERFECT PLAN OR ALL THE ANSWERS. MOVE FORWARD, MAKE MISTAKES, LEARN, AND ADJUST FOR THE NEXT STEP.

Chapter 12:

OFTEN TIMES YOUR GREATEST ABILITY CAN ALSO BE YOUR GREATEST WEAKNESS

"Contentment makes poor men rich;
discontentment makes rich men poor."
-Unknown

This is the toughest chapter for me to write. The issues discussed in this chapter could be the most important of all emotionally, spiritually and for sure financially. Have you noticed that oftentimes when people (especially men) become successful they tend to wear their arrogance like a shirt and start thinking and actually professing that "they deserve more?" They deserve a better home, a better car, better clothes, and worst of all, a better wife. It is almost comical to have to write about this because most of this book is about changing your mindset to believe in yourself. The key is to develop confidence in yourself but to remain humble and remember where you came from.

Coming from where I was to where I am, I was driven to always do more, have more and be more. I currently have an amazing home (size of it qualifies as a mansion), a garage full of super cars and all the other toys I could ever dream of but continue to struggle with contentment. One definition of contentment is a state of happiness and satisfaction. Somewhere along the path to success some of us get so wrapped up in achieving we forget or simply don't take the time to stop and be thankful for what we have. There is always a better car out there. I currently have what I thought was my dream car in a McLaren 720S but then I saw a McLaren Senna! The Senna is a one million plus dollar car. Who on earth needs a car that expensive? I set goals and tie rewards to the goal, which is great for motivation, but it causes me to be discontent having the three hundred thousand dollar 720S. Sounds completely idiotic doesn't it! Find a balance between keeping yourself motivated and enjoying the amazing blessings you have currently.

I hate long distance running but I wanted to get that 26.2 sticker that shows me and the world, I ran a marathon. After I ran a 5k, I began training to run a 10k, then a 15k and eventually a half marathon. The number of people that complete a half marathon is not that large but the minute I finished it, I was ready to move on to the full marathon. I did not give myself time to celebrate or enjoy my accomplishments to that point. I minimized the accomplishments to that point and moved on to focus on the full marathon. Guard yourself from doing this with other things in your life. Slow down a little to count your blessings. Things may be stepping stones but people are not. As you move along your success path you will grow and change. You are NOT better than the people in your life that have not changed.

I currently have four friends that have achieved a good level of success and are all in some stage of divorce. They all see themselves as hard working overachievers. They all have good personalities, have above average looks and take care of themselves physically to a degree. They receive constant praise from those in their work environment and then go home to the woman they have spent years with, including a large portion of the time they were not that successful. Their spouses are the same as they always have been but are not giving them the praise they get from the outside world. I have had multiple conversations with all of them as I experienced the same thing. The problem is not the spouse and their perceived lack of affirmation, the problem is our over-inflated sense of self.

You might be asking yourself, why is Paul talking about marriage issues in a financial book. The financial answer is simple. Why learn how to grow yourself to create wealth only to give one third to one half away to an attorney. More importantly, to help you guard against arrogance replacing thankfulness. Your efforts are something to be proud of but can be destructive if you allow yourself to become so prideful that you think you are better than those around you or those that were by your side and supporting you when you had very little to be prideful about. The Bible says, "Pride comes before the fall." God has given all of us the tools to be as successful as we want to be especially if you live in the United States. You are a masterpiece. Something for all the world to marvel at your abilities. Those of us that have fought the good fight to grow and change our life and the lives of generations to come must guard against learning the lesson of building greatness only to fail in life and love.

I am not saying it is wrong to be proud of who you become. You should be just as proud of yourself at the beginning of your journey as you are after you begin reaching your goals. As you focus on the effort to become successful, have pride that you are willing to put forth that effort but do not mistakenly think you are above others or deserve more than others. I laugh when I read stories of "famous" people that get stopped for speeding by the police. How often do they say, "do you know who I am?" What on earth does who they are have to do with the fact they broke the law. We have that same issue with politicians today. They make rules that do not apply to themselves because they believe they are better than every one else. You are special but you do not deserve special treatment.

My personality is a lot like Samson from the Bible. Samson was a warrior who kicked down the doors and took the plunder as his own. I grew up thinking that I cannot rely on anyone else. I did not need anyone else because if it was to be, I had to make it happen. If someone wanted to be with me great, if not their loss. Between my mom and dad, they totaled eleven marriages. Faithfulness and commitment were not a thing that was valued or taught in my family. No one in my family including both sets of grandparents stayed married.

My four friends all share several things in common with me. They all created success on their own through sheer force and perseverance. No one gave them a thing. They built and took what they needed to succeed. They began their family life before they became successful with the woman of their dreams. The common theme in this book is you will have to change who you are to change the life you have. Myself as well as my four friends are not the same men today that we were when we began our journey. The abilities and strengths to push ourselves toward success also allowed us to re-evaluate our lives after some success. The woman that used to hang the moon, who maybe didn't change like we had because they were not really involved with the businesses we grew, was seen as not being appreciative for what we had done. My mom used to say, "don't forget where you came from." A lot of us do indeed forget where we came from.

Lori and I started dating at age 15 and got married at age 19. I sincerely believed that I had married up and didn't deserve to have her. I came into our marriage with all the baggage of what I had learned from my family history. Lori on the other hand had a different experience. I believe she had one aunt that had divorced but all other family members remained married. She had grandmothers that lost their husbands and remained single for the rest of their lives. Till death do us part was something she learned. We started achieving a very good level of success in our early 40's and the "mid-life re-evaluation" hit. I changed how I treated her, and she reacted with complaints. I had the attitude that if she wanted to be treated like a queen, she should treat me like a king. I guess I thought I deserved to be one of those kings from medieval times, sitting on a thrown with Lori at my feet handing me grapes as I bellowed out commands.

I compared the respect and affirmation that others treated me with to how she treated me and formed a view of her that a lot of successful people do of their spouses. I saw her as ungrateful, unappreciative, and undeserving of me. I literally laugh today that I thought she was undeserving of me. The guy that very easily could have been an alcoholic, abusive, nonproductive member of society like most of my family. My attitude changed from believing how lucky I was to have married Lori, to believing that she did not deserve to be with me! I had become successful but almost lost everything literally and figuratively. In a typical divorce the husband and wife each get a third and the attorneys get a third. But more importantly the perceived short term "gain" of thinking I could find someone that more deserved me would have cost me the most amazing life possible with my family not to mention the catastrophic financial loss.

I found my solution to happiness and a balance of contentment and motivation to continue to grow the same way I have been teaching you to gain success in this book. I stopped and examined where I was then defined where I wanted, to be years from then. I sought the wisdom of those that had what I wanted including reading books on contentment. I developed a plan and jumped out of the airplane and assembled the parachute on the way down figuring things out as we went. During my journey to regain what was really important, I found out that most of the people that I asked, that had divorced, said they regretted it even if they said they were currently happy. The consensus was the affects on sharing kids, grandkids, holidays, birthdays and other "normal" parts of life was horrible, it set them back significantly financially, and after they "replaced" their spouse they figured out it was not better, just different. Whether it is your spouse, the next great car or home etc., if you don't take time to appreciate what you have you too will come to the realization that what is newer and more shiny isn't better it is just different. The benefit of getting the new most of the time is not worth the cost.

One of the people I sought out was a counselor named Dawn Marie Colaw. Once I laid my situation out to her, she said "so what you are saying is you DESERVE to be happy and to be treated in a manner you think is better and that Lori does not deserve your love any longer." I thought, finally someone who understands. Then she asked me if I had ever heard of this guy named Jesus. To which I replied of course. She then asked me if I knew what he did for me. I said you mean be beaten, tortured, and killed on a cross as a sacrifice for my sins. In her sweet little voice, she said what did you do to deserve his love and sacrifice? She could have hit me in the face with a baseball bat and it not hurt worse. In that moment and with that one question, I was brought back to reality. She knocked me off my arrogant pedestal and saved my marriage. It was like a drain that had been clogged was now running full force. I was immediately humbled to the point of disgust. I was so blinded by pride and full of myself, I lost sight of one of the greatest gifts I had been given by God.

Whether you are a Christian or even believe in God, the Bible is a guidebook for a happy and successful life. As my "clogged brain" was cleared, I began to remember important points from this guidebook of life like:

> -When people get married, two become one. Just like when people lose a leg or an arm, they have fantom pains, a divorced couple will have pains beyond financial as a divorce is a ripping of two that became one back into two;

> -The love of money is the rout of all evil;

> -What is it worth to gain the entire world and lose your soul;

> -Pride comes before the fall; and

> -God's plan for our life is better than our own plan (including the one I thought I deserved).

After my counseling session, I received a card from Lori at the apartment I had been living that read as follows:

> Lord,
>
> You've said that faith comes by hearing, and hearing by the word of God (Romans 10:17). I pray that you would feed Paul's soul with your word, so his faith grows big enough to believe that with you all things are possible (Mat. 19:26).
>
> Give Paul unfailing certainty that what you've promised to do, you will do (Romans 4:21). Make his faith a shield of protection. Put it into action to move the mountains in his life. Your word says, the just shall live by faith (Romans 1:17), I pray that Paul will live the kind of faith-filled life you've called us all to experience.
>
> May Paul know with complete certainty how great is your goodness which you have laid up for those who fear you, which you have prepared for those who trust in you (Psalm 31:19).
>
> In Jesus' name I pray
> Amen

God, through Lori and Mrs. Colaw, knocked me back on track to understand that happiness and contentment come from serving and loving unconditionally. The decision to not divorce and to submit to God's plan for my life was absolutely the best choice I ever made, including financially. I intentionally used the word choice because once again I proved to myself that my life is a direct result of my choices. I almost allowed the drive, tenacity, do it myself attitude that helped me achieve success to destroy the very life I had once dreamed of and had been pursuing. What allowed me to achieve success was the exact thing that almost destroyed it. I spent years of pain, suffering, struggle, extra hard work to build a magnificent "mansion of a life" to get to a point where I almost burnt it to the ground because of my pride.

I believe that God indeed has a plan for your life and if you humble yourself and slow things down to focus on what is important, he will prove to you that his plan is much better than yours. Guard yourself against yourself my friends. You will actually be more happy with the old car, the normal house and the woman that started out as the woman of your dreams. There is nothing more worthy of your extra effort than to protect your family from your pride. I saw a meme once that said, "Marriage is till death do us part, we failed today. Shut up, go to sleep and try again tomorrow." The principle that success is gained through small victories applies to your marriage and personal life as well. If things suck in your personal life practice all the steps we have discussed in this book. Don't blame others or your circumstances, take a very detailed inventory of yourself including your actions and reactions, define the type of personal life you want, study those that have that life, compare what you do to what they do, seek advice from others that have the "fruit on the tree", and gain small victories to reach success.

STEP #12: DON'T SPEND YEARS BUILDING THE FINANCIAL AND PERSONAL LIFE OF YOUR DREAMS AND THEN BURN IT TO THE GROUND BECAUSE OF PRIDE. DO NOT BECOME A "DO YOU KNOW WHO I AM PERSON."

Chapter 13:

NO MORE EXCUSES, IT IS TIME TO START

"Vision without Execution is Hallucination"
-Thomas Edison

The world is full of dreamers but has few doers. My hope is that this book will help more people to take their dreams of a better life and understand there is a predictable path to making them come true. You should not be judged by your race, your past, your sex, who your parents were or any other thing about yourself. The measuring stick of your life should be how you used the magnificent uniqueness that is you to impact the lives of those around you.

You have all the talents to be a game changer for your family and generations to come. As a man of faith, I believe the greatest sin of all is wasting the gifts that you have been given to improve the lives of your fellow men and women. Life, opinions of others, society biases, family, preconceived limitations, and fear destroy the joy and excitement of our childhood thinking that we can accomplish anything we want.

My friends, I know you without even meeting you. I believe in you, not from a "raw-raw" get all hyped up sense but from direct knowledge that you were created with potential beyond your comprehension. I look at my surroundings and am in awe at my life. I am no better or worse than you. I started from a position in life better than some of you and much worse than others. I set out to present a technical step by step plan (as a good accountant would) to get you from where you are to where you want to be. It is a road map to success that I learned from life experience of my own and from the lives of those that have come before me. My talent is simply being willing to "do before I know", never quit, and learn from those that have been willing to share their stories with me personally and through their books.

Success is left for all of us to define for ourselves. My hope is that you understand with zero doubt that you are where you are based upon the choices you have made to act or react to your circumstances. I acknowledge life is hard. The struggle is real but so is the solution. Will you change YOU and thus change the

lives of your generations to come? My friend I quote again….
"Success requires no apologies and failure allows no alibies."

The knowledge that I have learned and try to pass on to you is both very exciting and horribly depressing. You no longer have any excuses for not being successful. Your success or lack there of is all a direct result of your choices. Maybe so far you have been able to blame your lack of knowledge that a map exists, but no longer. I do not apologize for taking away your excuses because I know the potential in you and have seen the impact of those that embrace their potential and those that do not. You have gifts and talents that this world needs to experience.

I am just a guy walking on a beach with thousands of starfish washed up out of the ocean. They are all struggling to survive. Some are looking for a handout, but others just want a hand up. My hope is that those of you wanting a real solution to unlocking your potential accept this book as a hand up! You cannot measure the ripple effect in the lives of everyone that you care about. You are the key. Will you be the person that says no more excuses? I pray for you to have the strength of my mom who said no more alcoholism, no more abuse, no more slothfulness, no more blaming others, give me an opportunity and get out of the way. You got this…. Now get busy. Action creates motivation which creates passion.

Once again, the twelve-step road map that will create predictable success results for you are:

STEP #1: REALIZE YOUR PAST STRUGGLES MAKE YOU STRONG AND ARE NOT AN EXCUSE TO FAIL.

STEP #2: CHANGING YOUR THOUGHTS AND ATTITUDE IS THE MOST VITAL STEP TOWARD SUCCESS!

STEP #3: DEFINE WHERE YOU ARE AND WHERE YOU WANT TO GO, CREATE A PLAN TO GET THERE, AND MEASURE THE RESULTS AS YOU GO TO ALLOW YOU TO REFINE YOUR PLAN!

STEP #4: CLONE YOURSELF THROUGH THE USE OF DOCUMENTED PROCESSES, HIRE PROACTIVELY FOR ATTITUDE INSTEAD OF SKILL, AND PROACTIVELY CONTROL YOUR TIME.

STEP #5: A DOLLAR SAVED TODAY CREATES $1,000 IN THE FUTURE. SAVE AND INVEST AND LIVE ON LESS.

STEP #6: YOUR SUCCESS WILL BE ACCELERATED BY SEEKING THE WISDOM OF OTHERS THAT HAVE ACHIEVED THE SUCCESS YOU DESIRE. BE WARY THAT THEY INDEED HAVE ACHIEVED SUCCESS IN THE AREAS THEY ARE OFFERING ADVICE.

STEP #7: ALL SUCCESS BEGINS WITH YOU. BE PROACTIVE IN ASSESSING YOUR STRENGTHS AND WEAKNESSES THEN FOCUS ON IMPROVING YOUR BIGGEST ASSET, YOU!

STEP #8: GIVING IS THE KEY TO HAPPINESS AND CONTENTMENT. PLAN HOW YOU GIVE TO BLESS OTHERS, ENCOURAGE OTHERS TO GIVE, AND UNDERSTAND THERE IS RECIPROCITY IN GIVING.

STEP #9: DO A DEEP DIVE ON EVERYTHING YOU THINK AND KNOW. WHAT YOU KNOW YOU HAVE LEARNED FROM YOUR EXISTING ENVIRONMENT AND OFTEN TIMES PIGS DON'T KNOW PIGS STINK (INCLUDING WHAT THEY THINK IS TRUE AND FALSE ABOUT THE WORLD AROUND THEM).

STEP #10: CREATE A NO QUIT ATTITUDE BY BEING MANICALLY FOCUSED AND INTENTIONAL WITH EVERY DECISION YOU MAKE. FIGHT THE EASY CHOICES THAT LEAD TO DRIFTING AND FOR GOD'S SAKE, READ NAPOLEON HILL'S BOOK THINK AND GROW RICH MULTIPLE TIMES!

STEP #11: BE A READY, AIM, FIRE AND ADJUST PERSON. DON'T WAIT TILL YOU HAVE THE PERFECT PLAN OR ALL THE ANSWERS. MOVE FORWARD, MAKE MISTAKES, LEARN, AND ADJUST FOR THE NEXT STEP.

STEP #12: DON'T SPEND YEARS BUILDING THE FINANCIAL AND PERSONAL LIFE OF YOUR DREAMS AND THEN BURN IT TO THE GROUND BECAUSE OF PRIDE. DO NOT BECOME A "DO YOU KNOW WHO I AM PERSON."

Suggested Reading Supplement

This is not a complete list of the books that you will want to read but a very good beginning. In many of these books the authors will recommend other great books that influenced them. One last recommendation. When I read a book, I mark up the actual book then go back and type up my notes. This allows me to go back months later and read my notes to remind myself of the little nuggets. I know a lot of you will think that is overkill, but do you want the life of your dreams? What is overkill if it accelerates your path?

THE BIBLE BY GOD

ULTIMATE SALES MACHINE
by Chet Holmes

THE GREATEST MIRACLE IN THE WORLD
by Og Mandino

GOOD TO GREAT
by Jim Collins

RAVING FANS
by Ken Blanchard

THE ONE MINUTE MANAGER
by Ken Blanchard

LEADERSHIP AND THE ONE MINUTE MANAGER
by Ken Blanchard

THE ONE MINUTE MANAGER MEETS THE MONKEY
by Ken Blanchard

GUNG HO
by Ken Blanchard

THINK AND GROW RICH
by Napoleon Hill

OUTWITTING THE DEVIL
by Napoleon Hill

YOU CAN'T STEAL SECOND WITH YOUR FOOT ON FIRST
by Burke Hedges

HOW TO WIN FRIENDS AND INFLUENCE PEOPLE
by Dale Carnegie

HUNG BY THE TONGUE
by Francis P Martin

PERSONALITY PLUS
by Florence Littauer

QUICK TO LISTEN SLOW TO SPEAK
by Robert Fisher

SCALE
by Jeff Hoffman

THE RICHEST MAN IN BABYLON
by George Clason

GET OFF YOUR "BUT"
by Sean Stephenson

THE SUBTLE ART OF NOT GIVING A F*CK
by Mark Manson

EVERYTHING IS F*CKED
by Mark Manson

THE TRANSFORMATIVE CEO
by Jeffrey J. Fox

THE MILLIONAIRE MAP
by Jim Stovall

THE GIFT OF GIVING BY
Jim Stovall

THE ULTIMATE GIFT
by Jim Stovall

THE ART OF COMMUNICATION
by Jim Stovall

YOU DON'T HAVE TO BE BLIND TO SEE
by Jim Stovall

THE ART OF LEARNING
by Jim Stovall

THE ART OF ENTREPRENEURSHIP
by Jim Stovall

WHO MOVED MY CHEESE
by Spencer Johnson

EXTREME OWNERSHIP
by Jocko Willink

THE CHECKLIST MANIFESTO
by Atul Gawande

FISH
by Stephen Lundin

VISIONEERING
by Andy Stanley

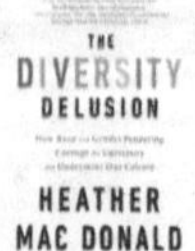

THE DIVERSITY DELUSION
by Heather MaDonald

THE ENERGY BUS
by Jon Gordon

THE WAY OF THE SHEPARD
by Kevin Leman

ENTRELEADERSHIP
by Dave Ramsey

UNLIMITED WEALTH
by Paul Zane Pilzer

THE ART OF GETTING THINGS DONE
by Clay Clark

UNFU*K YOURSELF
by Gary Johnson Bishop

NEVER SPLIT THE DIFFERENCE
by Chris Voss

WINNING
by Jack Welch

START WITH WHY
by Simon Sinek

MAXIMIZED MANHOOD
by Cole Edwin

THE OUTLIERS
by Malcolm Gladwell

SNOWBALL
by Alice Schroeder

OWN THE DAY, OWN YOUR LIFE
by Aubrey Marcus

TRACTION
by Gino Wickman

THE ART OF WORK
by Jeff Goins

www.ingramcontent.com/pod-product-compliance
Lightning Source LLC
Chambersburg PA
CBHW012032140726
47990CB00009B/3196